T0063432

THE Musical Soul TRAIN

Discover the Songs from Your Heart

PHILIP "PM" MOEY

PARTRIDGE

A Penguin Random House Company

To order additional copies of this book, contact
Toll Free 800 101 2657 (Singapore)
Toll Free 1 800 81 7340 (Malaysia)
orders.singapore@partridgepublishing.com

www.partridgepublishing.com/singapore

In memory of my late father, George Moey, who gave me the appreciation and love for music as he filled us with the possibilities of a great life, in simple gestures of love and non attachment to the physical excessiveness of the modern world.

Dedicated to my family for their love and support and allowing me to evolve into the person whom I have grown to be and realization that we are just a visitor in this vast expansion of reality we call life.

To my wife and three children, I leave these messages that have helped me navigate the waters of reality with the acknowledgment that we are never alone to experience life's tapestry of awe and wonders of creation. We need to celebrate life and serve humanity as your ultimate calling.

To the music lovers of the world, do not die with the music still in you. Sing the songs from your heart and live courageously. It is the universal language that transcends all cultures that brings peace to humanity.

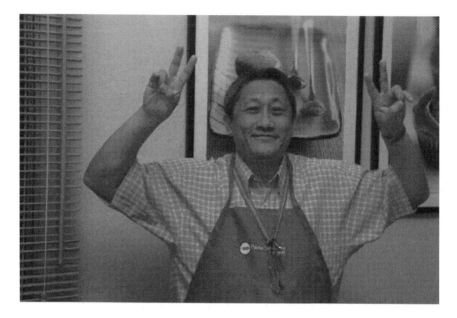

The author is cooking up a storm and is ready to feed you with many personal stories, insightful learnings on his journey towards spirituality and reflections on daily living and perhaps some nourishment for the soul as a dessert. Armed in red to the tee he appears pretty set to fire up the engines to start the ride on
The Musical Soul Train.

Welcome, be seated and buckle up to enjoy the journey with him. The train will be leaving the station in a few moments.

Contents

Preface

The 33rd Verse

One who understands others has knowledge
One who understands himself has wisdom
Mastering others requires force
Mastering the self needs strength

If you realize you have enough
You are truly rich

One who gives himself to his position
Surely lives long
One who gives himself to the Tao
Surely lives forever

Lao Tzu

This 33rd verse comes from the Tao Te Ching, notably one of the greatest books ever written and is entitled Living Self Mastery. This verse challenges us to look within ourselves and develop a sense of mastery by changing how we see the world and how our lives have been unfolding and the choices we adopt from the moment we were born into this physical realm till the time we are ready to return to where we came from. How we master our own lives by living extraordinarily will be a unique journey for each individual to undertake. Some may say living a good life is my goal, but you have the potential to live a great life if you choose to. As the saying goes the good is the enemy of the great. We have many good schools but a few great schools. We have many good companies, good governments but few are really great. Similarly many want a good life which is nothing wrong in itself but if you had a chance to live a great one, would you not want it. Life is what you make of it, and it is your choice how to make it work for you. This would be the ultimate goal for any human being to consider and for us to keep in mind of this possibility as we begin this journey of reflection to be in alignment with our pre-ordained destiny. At first glance it would be perceived that only the special few can achieve self mastery in the art of living but I believe the great master Lao Tzu is telling us that everyone is capable of doing it, only that we have not tapped into this potential within us. That is why this verse suggests we can attain wisdom in understanding thy self better and when we live by the tenets of the Tao (the origin source of spirit) it will guide our internal light towards eternal bliss and true happiness and be congruent to universal laws and principles. It is there for us to embrace. We just need to make a conscious decision to go to that place.

The concept of life is both intriguing as it is fascinating and sometimes downright complicated. I have realized that this journey on earth is what you make of it and it starts from the morning of life, from the time you are born, and what we went through in the early formative years that perhaps made the stamp on our nature. Most research says that up to six years of age the child's mind is at its fertile best to mold one's thinking patterns and eventually our character. I am sure that is a well documented possibility although I cannot recall my first couple of years of physical existence myself to validate that view, but from my own experience our character is a product of how we were taught to see the world. This was made possible by well meaning adults such as our parents, teachers and many others. These individuals who passed on their views of the world to us were probably molded themselves by their own parents and teachers, and we started to understand, see and perceive the world around us through a well laid out domestication process.

We started school life at about 7 years of age and for the next 12 years we navigated the many classrooms till the end of high school. We made many great friends and vowed never to be separated for the rest of our lives. Some did stay connected but many went separate ways when we left high school and went to college. Up till nineteen years of age, we were all called teenagers. When reflecting back, those were the really great and fun-filled years. Teens are teens and they do "teeny" things that parents never seem to understand. You should know. You were also a teen at a certain point in time. Seen that and done that phase. It is fascinating how easily we forget (or pretend to forget) our own experiences when we were at that age. When we did it, it seemed okay, but when we became parents ourselves, somehow the time warp changed us into another being altogether, and we disconnect with those emotions, and we often overly protect our children. I have three children and I saw first hand that beautiful phase of teenage-hood reappearing again and again. How many of us wished we could relive those moments. Those were carefree days and that made life worth living. Today with all efforts we put in, in striving to arrive, we may find that we are no better off in the quality of living. More conflicts, higher stress levels and pre-matured grey hairs (or complete absence of hair) came with the package of being an adult and making it in the world.

Then it was time to leave the nest of teenage bliss to take up a more serious view of the world and grow up into an adult and start to make a life for oneself. All of a sudden we needed to put up a more serious demeanor. Going to university was a likely prerequisite for many and to study a chosen vocation and then enter the working class. In university you found out that you could make more choices in the selection of subjects but it was up to you to be disciplined, matured and independent in your actions. Some of course took the road towards the university of "hard knocks" (street wise learning), and by no means of any lesser importance. It was just a different route for some of us.

We eventually entered the work force between the ages of 22 to 25 and earned our keep and then we became seemingly more independent, at least from the perspective that you no longer needed pocket money from your parents. You then engaged in your field of work for possibly the next 30 to 40 years attempting to make a mark and putting your stamp on the planet to say I am now here, watch me go, watch me soar. We scaled up the corporate ladder, fought tooth and nail to be noticed and reached a high point and then say "I have made it". Many take pride in placing their title and qualification on their name cards that were three times longer than their names. The corner office was a prized commodity. Some became their own bosses with a keen entrepreneurial spirit. In that illustrious journey you found out (some through the hard way) that you were not alone and you had to work with other people. You had to deal with and manage others and in the process you realized the immense complications in dealing with another human being (another body with 60 trillion cells). You started to understand the intricacies of inter-personal connections and in developing strong relationships and establish a desired network of friends and business associates. Some worked out well while others you rather not talk about. You also realized that the few great friends you have are a handful, while the rest always appear when you are on the rise and quickly disappear when one is down and out. Strange how this attraction works out, like bees attracted to honey.

In your mid 50s, coming into the afternoon of life some will begin to slow down and look forward to some form of retirement and bliss. Many people I have met worry about this phase. "What am I going to do" they ask? We may tend to feel a little helpless and perhaps a pinch at the EGO, especially for those who are coming out of the corporate setting where they were waited on hand and foot, with personal assistants and company driver, and often travel business or first class. Suddenly all the hoops and whistles and associated perks stopped. Could be quite a drama acting out upon retirement. We may think of travelling more for leisure but this can only be temporary, or to chill out every day at the "kopitiam" (the local version of Coffee Bean) with nothing important on our minds and look forward to the daily happenings and local gossips. After a while we may feel downright bored and start looking for some new action. I know friends who take up golf or gardening to occupy that space. Some find solace in front of the computer several hours a day keeping in touch with the happenings in cyber space and blogging out. This is fine as long as you are happy with it. Then before you know it, we approach 60s and eventually hit the twilight years in the 70s and 80s. Many say as we grow older we grow wiser. Very possible, but some just get older, period. What you do with your life, your actions, decisions and commitments from the time you are capable to think for yourself will mold your journey and even one's destiny. It is up to you to take necessary action. It is never too late to do this. You have much to give to your family, society and humanity. It is practically only a thought away. Ponder upon this.

From the time of your birth till now in your current stage of life, whether you are in your 20s, 50s or 70s, you would have encountered various experiences, some seemingly normal and others more purposeful. For me it was not until I was in my 40s I took stock of my "being here" and started reflecting what was my purpose on this planet? Who put me here and why? Apart from the fact my father and mother "did it" and I was the intended result of that act, and therefore here I am. And is it all over when death comes knocking and our body returns to dust! This had led me to look back and ask what were the messages and learning points so far in this journey. Well to be honest it did not seem like a journey then as each passing day came upon waking and was gone when the sun set, and the day was just another day, and the same old grind week after week, year after year. The 40 years that went by was like a flash and this had me pondering what would I make of my life the next 40 years if I am permitted to be still around. When you start connecting the dots you find that there was a pattern but you had no clue how it would have worked out for you. You had just travelled the road that many choose as the safe route, and fewer on the road less travelled. By nature we always use the same route, and by deliberately changing the path one day you begin to see other things and have fresh experiences.

Using the analogy of a long train ride, I knew I had crossed paths at many stations before, but did I stop to appreciate these stations of life or was I in a hurry to get to my next destination (whatever that was). When in school we dreamt of entering the work force as quickly as possible. Parents guided their children to study a skill that earned big bucks. Some parents will tell their kids to study hard or you will "end up being a road sweeper". Everyone is chasing a qualification to compete in the world, and others even swear a double degree is the minimum to enter the job market. When we eventually settled in a vocation the next destination was to find a life partner and settle down. After that it was to own your first home. Before you know it, "little feet" came along and you had to secure their future as well. And the list goes on and you can easily fill in the rest of the journey yourself.

In the final analysis, what was my ultimate destination anyway? Did I know it for sure? Perhaps I could have even dozed off or slept through some stages of life and never even comprehended any wisdom or awakening, and that is the reason I am rewinding my path and taking a closer look at the various points of my life and recollecting thoughts and experiences to map out this path as clearly as I can. We go through life in a dash from one point to the other, and we have forgotten the journey and the memories of the trials and tribulations and the excitement of joyful events. The memories can only benefit us by allowing us to move forward. The past is the past and will not change but you can change from this moment on. The decision starts right here right now. At this very moment make that choice to live as you have been or to venture into the life of extra-ordinary living. It is no more than ordinary people doing extra-ordinary things with their life.

The stations represented in the following content of this book are various reflections from my personal vantage point and no matter what is your current stage in life, whether you are just a student, or already in the workforce or even a retiree, this sharing is relevant because all the stations offer its own unique reflective and learning perspective and are ultimately universally connected to each other as we progress through life. Some of these experiences come from observations I have made both in my own life and that of my family and also with acquaintances on a personal and professional level in the last four decades participating in the glorious maze of living life on this planet. I must also acknowledge all those beautiful people who have crossed my path and the many wisdom teachers who have taught me great insights and gave me a fresh view to see a new paradigm of possibilities in this remarkable world we live in. This became a reality because I became a student again at the young and tender age of 40 and spent the next 15 years thereafter in exploration and allowed the universal energy to show me the way.

Little did I know that when I launched an intention to learn more and open my heart to a greater wisdom many "dots" unfolded and began to turn up in front of me.

One such teacher that appeared was in the teachings of Lao Tze, a great sage from China who gave teachings of the TAO, which is also the WAY. He places the wisdom of living in 81 short verses which we will discuss later in the book. The WAY can be seen as the path to the truth, which is a fascinating proposition to view life. His 33rd verse, Living Self-Mastery, opened the chapter of this book.

When the student is ready the teachers started to appear. When I launched this vision to be in acceptance, the messages and learning came to me in the books that I read and the people that I met. Somehow the attraction happened and I did not know how then but I have a better clue today. It is a fact and I can attest to it. When you humble yourself and take each day as a new learning experience you will see many things that were originally blindsided by your ego. You also come into contact with many persons who are your teacher in more ways than one.

Another of my favorite wisdom teachers, Dr. Wayne Dyer had taught me along the way, was "to sell your cleverness and purchase bewilderment". We have been so highly "educated" to a point we feel we have known it all and seen all there is to see and we label ourselves as "cleverer", not realizing we know only a fraction of the truth. There is another sharing of this fact in the **Ho'oponopono** teachings which will be revealed later on in the journey. The signs are all out there and you need to open your inner vision (some refer to as the 3rd eye) to recognize it. Many will miss opportunities towards this path of wisdom not because they want to, but because they do not see them as such. By opening our minds and hearts to embrace renewed learning towards self mastery of our lives, we share a common story with everyone of its immense possibility to be a renewed person to live an extra-ordinary life. This is also your story waiting to be lived and told. My best wishes to one and all to fulfill your destiny on board your own soul train.

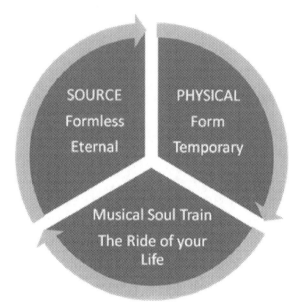

Inside the diagram:

SOURCE
Formless
Eternal

PHYSICAL
Form
Temporary

Musical Soul Train
The Ride of your
Life

Introduction: My Story

Quote:

*A journey of a thousand miles begins
with the very first step.*

INTRODUCTION

My Story

The Birth of a book and its title . . .

I have always been intrigued by the writers who could produce a well crafted book or a screenplay. It was unimaginable how they could have mustered so much material to tell their story. It seemed such a distant project that I could not imagine even doing one, but I harbored a silent wish of being a writer one fine day. However, some years ago, I came across this concept of a great life you can make for yourself and one of the dimensions you focus on was about leaving a legacy. That would have simply meant, reflecting on what we have done in this lifetime to leave this world a better place than when we first stepped on board on this mother ship called planet earth. I thought then a legacy would be so much more meaningful if there was a story behind it. Each person has a unique story only known to himself and is often kept as a silent unknown fact that he takes to his grave. We may feel that our lives have been ordinary but there are times we have experienced extra-ordinary events and insights or met wonderful people along the way which could be shared and perhaps learnt by others. Likewise we have also stumbled and picked ourselves up and learnt a lesson or two that have made us a little wiser or awakened to the episode. When I put pen to paper I could share some stories and insights of my life here on planet blue, and at the very least my children could see what went on in their old man's grey matter between his ears all these years. Good, great or otherwise, at least it would be my story! I started to write down short experiences and learning insights the last 10 years in scrap books and other media covering anything from my growing up years, family experiences, insights to new concepts and practices in daily living from new age thinking philosophies, my personal spiritual journey to understand who we are and the various sources of leadership material I had used in my training and development work in the corporate environment the last 25 years.

But I had not had the inspiration to put it all together until this moment, and by the grace of the almighty power of source spirit that have now awakened my soul and allowed me to connect the dots after 58 years of existence, this private book project had started to move forward and today is in print. As you are reading this, it is a testimony that the dream has become a reality and the promise I made to myself a long time ago to write a book one day has been fulfilled. I believe this calling comes to us in the quiet contemplations of life and amidst the many calming and reflective moments in the wee hours of the morning when most people in my part of the world are still asleep, when one is in-spirit, you get inspired thoughts that flow through you to the page.

I must admit that one of the final trigger points came upon my non coincidental stumbling on a book entitled ZEN guitar a few months back. This book was written by a guitarist musician finding his place in the sun and talks about the song that is inside us that is waiting to be played and discovering a path to give us spiritual fulfillment as music lovers. The preamble of this book was simply that we all carry a song inside us, and it is this song that makes us human. Somehow we never learnt how to unlock this song. This song is inside everyone and it does not matter if you are a shower singer, a basic 3-chord guitarist or a professional. This resonated so clearly with me due to my own love for music, as a self taught musician from my high school days, and having combined this love with the wider readings on literature of the modern day wisdom teachers, and molded with my life experiences, the book title became clearer to me as the days progressed.

So the journey started and what better representation I thought than seeing it as a train ride of your life. Trains have a magical and nostalgic touch as they travel far and wide, chugging along with their whistles blowing as if to announce to the world of their arrival and allowing passengers to have time to marvel at the sights, smells and sounds of the towns and countryside they pass and the stations they come to rest and refuel. The image of the Orient Express came to mind as I pondered on the book title, an elegant way of travel which is not rushed but headed in a pre-chosen destination. On board we have the luxury to enjoy all the amenities and this could represent what everyone wishes in his own life journey. The chosen word "soul" comes from a deeper realm of being with an understanding and representation that we are a delicate combination of form and formless energy. The formless divine presence represents an eternal reality that is not always seen nor felt but always pulsating and living. The presence of the soul inside us seem to tell me that, "I have been here before and it feels familiar", and perhaps it is now a right time to share the excitement of the unseen side as a mirror of the physical world we have grown to know so well.

Thus the SOUL TRAIN wordings were shortlisted for consideration. A further reflection will allow one to interpret the title as "training of one's soul" in this physical plane or "an invitation to join me in my journey on this train ride to explore what life is all about through my eyes". You too may have other insights as we journey together and that would be perfectly alright, because you may have your own realization unfold before your very eyes. All of us were brought into this world in various cultures and born of separate parents but a thought that we are also connected from a source of being is also a very viable proposition worth exploring. I am not a research scientist nor a great philosopher to prove this theory of oneness but have seen glimpses of its possibility in my interactions within a multi racial society that I come from and the people whom I have the privilege to know in my own journey so far. In particular when I observe children at play I am in awe of this openness and acceptance of each other which we all had once upon a time when we were children but perhaps had lost this essence in our growing up years.

If so why did this happen? Where has this child-like innocence gone and can we ever bring it back and have love in our hearts and acceptance for all we meet. Today with the world in its greatest period of momentous changes we need to find an answer before it is too little and too late.

The merging of the word "musical" in the final full title of this book was a natural conclusion, inspired by ZEN guitar writings and my own musical love story. This was instrumental (forgive the pun) to show that life is a song that is always in your heart, waiting to be sung. When you unlock this song, you begin to see the world in perfect harmony and splendor and to be living it accordingly. Life is what you make of it. If you see it as tough and vicious you are probably right, but if you see it otherwise you are also probably right too. As you think, so shall it be and it makes your reality. Your thoughts are extremely powerful energy forms and it shapes your life more than you know it. Either way I welcome you, the reader, to be on board and may you find your spot in the world that you too find your own pathway and can make a difference moving from ordinary levels of awareness to a higher plane of wisdom. Thank you for having included this reading into your lives. Please enjoy the *musical soul train*.

In the Beginning . . .

I have chosen to begin this book by sharing some background of my early life particularly by the deeper influences of my late father who have shaped my thinking by his own life examples even though it was not apparent some 25 years before this writing. I believe that each person who comes into our lives is by an intricate design of fate and there are no mistakes in God's pathway, and which we should open our hearts and eyes to observe and learn the wisdom of the ages and those who have come before us. How my father lived gives a glimpse of a man who had alternate values and showed me a way that I could consider emulating in my own time here on planet earth. Allow me to begin this personal journey with you. This is the story of my late father, and I dedicate this opening chapter to . . . .

My Dad,

If today were the 10th of March 2012 it would have been my Dad's 99th physical birthday, if he were still alive. Mr. George Moey Liang Teck, my late father, was a proud man, and in his early years he was a sport person and a keen body builder. When I was in my early teens, he bought me a Weider body building kit set. I remember that my friend JOHNNY Wong would come to pump weights in my tiny room every evening for as long as I can remember.

Johnny would be looking at the mirror in my room in Section 11 in PJ and admiring his "Pak Chum Kai" (in Cantonese dialect) somewhat a metaphorically translation for a fair and skinny physique. He was a highly disciplined fellow wanting to develop his muscles but results eluded him somehow, at least to my eyes.

Today reflecting on life, my regret was that I did not spend more time talking to George Moey to learn his wisdom. As a teenager I had my own world to navigate and master, and time with family was perhaps an outing and a weekend meal expedition. I had school to contend with, my sports activities, my school band and of course girlfriends, so my time was fully occupied. Now I know better, as I had probably missed the precious opportunity to learn his wisdom firsthand. In a way he was a man of few words. He nevertheless left me with the knowledge that we can always be happy when we have family around us and his passion for wanting to celebrate whenever we could, not in a grandeur manner, but a simple but elegant meal whenever he had made some money after his card games at the SCRC (Selangor Chinese Recreation Club) in KL town. I used to meet him there after school to catch a ride home, and his famous words were, "today made some money and we can have some good makan (meal)", and off we went with the family.

The restaurant we frequented had a pre set menu because we always ordered the same few dishes, no mistake! It was a corner coffee shop place in PJ new town and Hong Siew Yee Tau (a fish head dish with assorted vegetables) was the pick of the day. In fact the captain knew our preferences by heart, as it was almost the same few dishes, like kang kong belachan (a local spicy vegetable dish), egg fuyong, hotplate taufoo, well at least we *were highly consistent in our choices. Other favorite places we frequented were DEVI, an Indian restaurant in Brickfields for banana leaf rice and on some grander occasions we would be in The Coliseum, the famous western food outlet in Jalan Tuanku Abdul Rahman. Favorite pickings were T-bone steak and pork chops, with sauteed onions, one large bowl . . . Yummy! He used to tell me this was the place when he himself went as a boy and 50 years on it is still there. At the time of writing The Coliseum is still operating, under new management but none of the older souls are around anymore.*

Mr. George Moey was one who lived his life filled with music in him, even though he needed some warm up time upon waking up in the mornings. No one dared speak to him as he was in his own sanctuary. He was like a grizzly bear just out from winter slumber. After some warm up he would pick up his guitar and played away. Even then it was the same few songs.

My knowledge of him was that of an honest and hardworking man. Hearing his early days in the service where he was at customs and later distributing land to new settlers in PJ new town, he could have easily kept a lot of properties for himself, but he did not. Not one single property. Living in Ampang Road in government quarters, my vivid recollection was in this large bungalow house where we need not lock the doors and we had no fencing in between the houses. My memory was that we had a large garden and my grandmother grew vegetables and papaya trees in the backyard. Those papayas were the best I have tasted, and she really had green fingers. Sometimes for lunch we just plucked some fresh green chillies and had them for lunch. The front side of the house has a large compound and on one of my birthdays I had a real life horse to ride on. It was a white little pony and yes, gang-nam Ampang style already started in those days.

Dad was also a stickler for no nonsense favoritism as he asked my sister to stand in line to collect our rations of rice during the Japanese war in the 1940s. His motto was fairness to all. This drove my mother up the wall as I was told. I was too young to know, probably not even born yet.

Dad was in government service and always came home for lunch for an hour and then back off to work. He had a driver named NAVI who had a canny resemblance of the king of rock, Elvis, was my recollection. At that time dad owned a Volvo. I learnt later that many thought him as a show off with a driver but the reality was that my dad had a condition where he felt sleepy at the wheel, which led him to get a driver for safety reasons. So lesson learnt was never to assume what is the reality behind each action.

A passion for cars—Mr. Moey senior changed cars practically every one to two years. In an uncanny way, mum was the famous lottery winner and funded his passion for new cars. He probably had 20 cars in all, and too many for me to name here. The one I remember was the Allegro or what I called the KeleGro (never knew why but sounded cool I suppose). Then there was the Humber Hawk, where you needed two hands to change gears. It was like a tank and probably would have had a concealed cannon somewhere, I swear.

Dad was a self taught musician and he played the harmonica, ukulele, guitar and the piano. Wherever he went he would be tickling the ivories. What he taught me as I now celebrate today his legacy was honesty and never be afraid of hard work. He said as long as you are diligent you will not go hungry. Today I can proudly dedicate a special room of musical instruments to his name and what a thrill dad would have been if he could see all this. But I believe he knows from his current vantage point, somewhere out there and the music of life continues to play on.

Dad had no accumulations of wealth and property and probably no desire to do so. When he retired he spent some 3 months on a world tour with my mother. Many of his contemporaries bought homes, but he saw it fit to see the world and that he did. I was too young to remember all the details. When dad left the government service we moved to private residences, starting with ChoTeck flats in Jalan Imbi, then Setapak Hot springs where I remember waking at wee hours to catch the bus to primary school. We later moved to PJ side in section 11, then to SS2 and finally to Kelana Jaya, a house my sister bought. Mum was the rock that survived all the moves, as she did the packing single handedly. When I bought my own home in Wangsa Baiduri, in Subang Jaya, mum was elated. All the trauma of moving house was finally over. Unfortunately dad never saw my new home. He passed away from a massive heart attack in Kelana Jaya. That was 25 years back in the mid 1980s.

Today as I become more in awareness of the greater wisdom of life, I can clearly admire that dad understood the temporal nature of materialism and accumulations. As we come to this planet we were born with nothing, we also bring nothing when we die. Instead of seeking such physical treasures, we should be building up good deeds by serving and giving with an abundance mindset and a loving heart. What we have today is already a blessing, with a healthy body and ability to earn a living and enjoy the journey.

We were married in that house in Kelana Jaya, a township 20 km from the city center, in 1982 and dad was with us when we had Terence and Tracy. He named Terence, our first born after the actor Terence Hill. On his passing Terence was four and Tracy was just one year old. It was 4 pm and we were all home as it was a Saturday afternoon. At an instant he was no more with us. I believe that he went the way he would have wanted, as he despised being locked up in hospitals, with tubes in him and on machines. This I believe was his blessing based on the life he led. Today as I am a little older and hopefully wiser, I begin to understand that the people whom we meet are defined for us as teachers and are there to guide us to be better persons. On a personal note, make a point to cherish all your loved ones because today is perhaps the best time to tell them you love them. Do not miss the last bus. Dad was always strong and proud and he taught me to stand for my rights. His key traits were honesty and he embodied what I know today as a person who did not dwell in materialism but nevertheless always provided for us in his best way possible.

Thank you dad for the love and legacy you left me and for the time spent with us. Today marks the 25th anniversary of your return to the origin of spirit and we are richly blessed by having you with us in this lifetime. God bless your soul. Your children and grand children are all making a life of their own and these blessings have come from the grace of God and the love of the ancestors of the MOEY lineage.

Happy Birthday dad! Today on the 10th March I remember your life and I am a better person having known you and was destined and privileged to be a part of this family.

As we progress in life we hope to be an example to the younger generation by our deeds and our actions. I believe that everyone is a God-given soul and deserves the right to be his own person. As parents we are only custodians to our children on a temporary basis and are here to provide a nurturing platform for growth and independence, as another child of God in this cycle of birth and rebirth. We pray each day we are able to be useful instruments to be God-like and think what he thinks, which is based on love and strictness built on universal laws and principles.

Thank you dad for having come into my life, and gave me a gift of love and wisdom.

Your loving son,
Philip

Mr. Moey Liang Teck, the late father of the author, in his hey days, on the electric guitar and playing out his music of life.

Today we will start this journey and we will be stopping at several stations along the way. I call these the ***stations of life and reflections*** which I have had the immense privilege to stop, stay a while, ponder, learn and soak in the wisdom that has made me a better person than what I was before. Some station stops were short and sweet filled with God's gifts, while others took more time as the wisdom of the teachings required greater refueling time and contemplation. I profess that it was not immediately an "aha" moment and sometimes the situations got the better of me. I could not see the profound messages in front of me. Ever felt like reading a book and you got almost nothing out of it, and a second reading later, it was perfectly clear. My only simple answer is that the time was not right for you. With persistence, I began to find the light and the wisdom of the learning that came with each event and encounter. At times you wondered if this is worthwhile as the going was tough and even lonely because you felt you were the only one thinking this way. In one of the journeys, I came across a teaching that said you are an unpolished diamond. You come from the earth all covered with impurities and yet there is a shining brilliance deep inside you. The key is not to find something better outside of you, but to uncover the wrappings that have polluted us over the centuries across many eons of humanity. Until you allow yourself to be scrubbed constantly you will never become a shiny stone. In life there are no easy rides, no shortcuts, and no groupon vouchers to buy. It is and always will be a life of waves and nodes, ups and downs. I choose to write these down as I see them to share with whoever is interested to take this ride, and as you read these reflections and experiences, I welcome you to join me and if it touches you somehow (even a tiny bit in your heart) it would have been worth my while and I am truly honored to have made this reading available to you. Each one of us has a story to tell and I am telling mine here as a legacy to my family and friends, on how the world has unfolded and what it has meant to me through my eyes, mind, heart and spirit.

As a ready born again student of life I openly welcome my teachers who are as varied as they are enlightened and are there for me constantly as long as I am ready to learn. Those folks who pushed your hot button, who got on your nerves were also your greatest teachers. They come in various forms and sizes, ranging from spouses, children, bosses, workmates, soul mates and the nice chap that honked at you this morning on your way to office for no apparent reason or the tea lady who had a sour face when you greeted her. They nourished your soul and strengthen your spirit. Every day is a new experience and a journey to be enjoyed. The destination was already known the minute I was born, that I was destined to die one day, and return to where I came from. But the unknown is the journey itself between these two points and the time span of this journey is not ours to call. The length of the railway track that the soul train rides on for each one is pre-destined. Let us hope that we do not run out of tracks before we visit all the beautiful stations of life. So welcome and Bon Voyage!

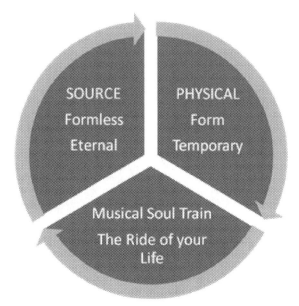

SOURCE
Formless
Eternal

PHYSICAL
Form
Temporary

Musical Soul Train
The Ride of your
Life

Station 1: Welcome Aboard

Quote:

*O Love, this is my song, this is a
song I sing to you*

STATION ONE

Welcome aboard

Today I stand in the middle of my music studio and I am gazing over my equipment, from the ivory beige Ibanez semi solid guitar, the oak wood Custom acoustic guitar, several Laney amplifiers and the conga/bongo combination. Among these pieces lies also a Hartke acoustic booster, a ZANGO beat-box machine and somewhere in the corner a bass guitar with a Line 6 bass amplifier, amidst a Fender PassPort 300 PA system and enough microphones and mike stands for a 5 man band. In the other room resides a full range 88-key Casio Electone organ and a recently purchased Korg PA500 performance keyboard, par excellence, I must say so myself. The KORG was a Christmas present given to me from me (you should try this sometime, it's great). To compliment this new addition, a pair of BEHRINGER Active 200 watt speakers were brought in together with a 12 channel mixer to exemplify the sound stage. I would have gotten a larger wattage pair of speakers but I was forewarned that the flooring and walls were not reinforced for sonic boom conditions and no special insurance was taken in the building. Talking about speakers, getting a 500 watt model is not meant to be louder in decibels but to be richer in sound reproduction. Just like in life, as you garner experiences (your wattage increases so to speak) and success does not call for you to be more superior to others (loud and booming). The larger wattage is used to signify higher awareness of being, potential to be more than what you

1

can be, calmness in thoughts and have clarity in your endeavors and the silent wisdom that you display.

Unless you are a musical buff like me these descriptive names on models and jargon may sound alien to you and is of little significance. If you are a little somewhat perplexed by the description of the various gizmos mentioned may I suggest you see this musical congregation of sorts as one of the re-fuelling depot for the musical soul train where the journey will start from and will also return to every now and then! As we navigate the journey of life we will be faced with many challenges and sometimes seems too hard to bear. This is the same analogy as hearing loud and screaming music and we must tone them down to meaningful levels for the greater appreciation of music. We must always be mindful that nothing that happens is by coincidence. Each encounter we face has a learning point embedded in the event and we must look for it. As for me, when the week is over and I feel exhausted, I will find solace in my music room. This is one place I return to be refueled, detached from the 10,000 things and be re-energized. Music has the power to move mountains but also soothe nervous energy. When I play one of the instruments I am in the moment and for that time period that is all that I am tuned-in to. Each instrument has its own character and the potential to make great music, and we are the catalyst to make it happen and make it come to life.

I have been challenged more than once by my better half, on why does one single person need so many musical instrumentation and gadgets. I wonder myself sometimes, but you know what, I have no regrets. My collection started in 2010 and after two plus years I have two rooms filled with musical magic, waiting to be played and enjoyed in all of its' splendor. Yes, all these equipment represent the varieties of life that we need to use as a vehicle as part of our kit in exploring our horizons. Each musical instrument will resonate a unique sound and gives us immense joy in the magical melody it gives out when played with oneness of the human spirit. Even the simple tambourine and castanets have a role in the musical world. I had dedicated this room to my late father who himself was a passionate musician, playing in cabarets in the 1950s. So did my inclination for music come from this source of being that came into my life? Possibly so! No, it is definitely so.

As I began my existence on planet earth somewhere in mid 1955, I vaguely remember my childhood days. The first five years were a hazy blur, I must admit but I can recall my nursery days going to kindergarten in Imbi Road and singing a song each morning to the teacher. At the tender age of 10, I got my first formal lesson in attempting to master the violin. My violin teacher Mr. Gomez, bless his soul, was a truly patient man. My father told me that the violin was the most difficult instrument to master and I had to learn reading notes as well. For those who may not feel the magic of this instrument, it is a weapon of sorts in the hands of the uninitiated. After 6 months I said goodbye to Mr. Gomez and hung up my strings. I could hear the neighbors rejoicing as their ears were spared the agony from the hours of scales practice on the violin. Actually it sounded like slaughtering well-fed chickens as I practised the scales daily after school. That was my one and only formal music training ever. Today I play by ear and do not read one iota of notes (as it has been dutifully returned to the teacher). The one lesson from my late father that sticks with me till this very day is that you pick and learn a song, memorize its chords and feel the beat, and you practise it 100 times, until it becomes part of you. It's like moving from unconscious incompetency to unconscious competency. Once you get it, it touches you and resides in your soul. Music has that magical power to fill you up. Music transcends all languages, all ethnic groups, all ages and gender. Playing a reflective piece in the quiet of the evening or early morning before dawn has a calming spiritual effect. As I write these words down I am listening to a spa musical piece that is soulful and enchanting. It fills up and warms the soul, and the clarity of thinking emerges flawlessly.

Growing up in a musical family, with my sister and niece also playing the piano and my late father on his acoustic guitar, we made a fair bit of musical sounds in our home. Additionally, I can recall as clear as day, the daily rituals my father had in the mornings. When my father awoke, he did not connect with anyone until he had his "wake-up ritual" of self connection. Upon waking, he (my dad) would walk downstairs and settle in his favorite chair at the corner overlooking the porch, lighting up a cigarette and picking up his acoustic guitar. It was as if the day had to start with a music prayer of some sort manifested through the guitar gods. All these rituals were never questioned, and only after playing a couple of songs, did he acknowledge others within 10 meters of where he sat. So this was a man with a wake-up routine, with a large mug of coffee, cigarette at the corner of his mouth and his guitar serenading the airwaves. Recently I picked up an interesting book reading entitled ZEN guitar. I was at a bookshop in Singapore and I was led to this section on philosophy and this book came to my attention as if it was waiting and calling for me. The title caught my eye and the book came home with me. Now I begin to understand the connectedness between a guitar player and his trusted instrument. A musician and his instrument are one in spirit and together come a gift of music that transcends the ordinary sounds we mortals hear every day. It feeds their souls and warms the heart. I have heard of similar connections that a kendo master has with his kendo sticks. The night before a competition, the kendo exponent sleeps with his trusted sticks before doing battle the next day. The master and his tools of trade are then in one spirit. So on competition day we see the masterful connection of a sifu (great master) and his trusted application of choice, his kendo sticks as one body.

Consistent with the music tradition that seems to flow in my veins, I began to pick up the drums. My late father had bought a hand-me-down set which was later sold to another aspiring musician who today is well known in music circles. We were staying in a single storey home with a large garden that served as a natural sound barrier (which was wishful thinking then) from the neighbors. No one talked about sound proofing, and never heard about it in those days. I remember very clearly that there was a symphony of mahjong tiles and drum beats in primal mode in that home. The house had a front and back portion and my mother and her friends always had a weekend dose of bonding over a four by four feet table and a box of mahjong tiles that went "clickati-click". They always occupied the back end, nearer the kitchen and we were left to take the living room area up front, where we had the piano, drums and acoustic guitars. I could swear that the aunties were challenging the drum beats each time they "washed" and re-arranged the mahjong tiles. Those were the days steeped in my memory and the beginning of my musical journey. As any 15 year old warm blooded individual surrounded with live sounds, I became part of the school band and partook in many talent time competitions. However with all that talent oozing out I never remember winning any prizes. Strange but true and I can only relate this to slightly tone deaf judges. So music filled my early years. Then 25 plus years in between was a hiatus as we were consumed with the traditional fulfillment of a career, family building and chasing the success of life linked to titles, accomplishments, possessions and feeling important. It was very interesting how all these formed the priorities in the morning stages of life, the ambitions and adventures we chased and what I thought that I have finally arrived. Little did I know then these would change drastically in my later years in the afternoon of life, and reflecting perhaps we had just started on the "real" journey.

Although the physical song playing and instrumental connection stopped for many years, I had unknowingly moved into another level of musical wonder, which were the songs that tugged at the heart strings. I would love to share this journey and invite you to join me on the musical soul train. If you decide to leave us now, we thank you for staying on this far. When you feel like rejoining the journey you are welcome anytime to hop on the soul train at our next station. As for the rest, please come back on board.

The soul train begins to warm up in readiness to leave the 1st station . . . .

The growing up years

Along with many young teens whose journeys are probably similar even today, I was put through the mill to finish high school and moved on to higher education, choose a career that makes good money and enter the work force preferably with a good solid company. I did enter the job market very early on immediately after high school and my first job was in a local bank. Those days a bank job was the crème de le creme job for many. I was told that to climb the corporate ladder in the bank you should pursue a banking diploma which enabled one to rise to the ranks of junior officer. With that engrained motivation of a life long career in banking, I manage to stay exactly 10 months and I dismissed my boss un-shamefully and chose a path to study accountancy. Why accountancy? Why not? Every company needs an accountant, that was what I was told. This decision did not go down well with my father as he had pulled many strings to place me in the bank. I had started my work career in the personnel department of the bank under one Mr. Lye PY. Those days in the 1970s the term human resources was not conceived yet.

Anyway working in the bank was memorable and one of my great joys was to own a brand new Yamaha 100 cc bike, colored red with black stripes and was spanking new. It was the thrill of freedom and felt great with the wind in my hair riding that new bike. I felt like I had the keys to the world. However, my joy lasted a short 8 months as my new bike was stolen from the banking compound, supposedly under guard in the bank premise. When you presumably lose something it can only be stolen or repossessed and I am quite sure it was not the latter. My recollection was a "lump" in your throat when you could not locate your possession even though you could have sworn this was the place you parked it that very morning. After some frantic walk about, you somehow get the sinking feeling that it is no more there. Ever experienced this feeling? This made me realize that nothing of a material nature is permanent, even though it was a hard hit lesson in my early years. As a young man of 20 this was not an insightful revelation at that point but more of anger and frustration and the thought of unfairness of the one above. However, this was lesson one on the temporary nature of things.

The Music of Life

The symphony of life started to bloom when I married my girlfriend whom I had known already for 7 years while in college and we soon started our family. Being of Asian heritage we had absolutely no qualms living under the same roof with my parents. My son and daughter were a gift to us soon after and our band started to grow. Seeing them evolving as tiny tots to walking beings was a magical time. My first two children also experienced the musical prowess of their grandfather. The house was filled with piano pieces and guitar strumming during the day. Indeed the music filled our lives. Ten years after my first born, we were again blessed with a son, our third child, but he did not get to appreciate his grandfather's musical talent and humor. His only references today to that generation (the life of my late father) are the photos that adorned my music studio today. My music studio that currently occupies two rooms in my home is dedicated to my father, George Moey, to remember him as a dutiful husband, father and grandfather and his spirit of living life full and as a passionate human being who had a heart of service, lives on amidst my musical sanctuary today. There are several photos of my late father, one strumming an electric guitar and one on the piano. I even have one of him doing the cha cha dance, or some form of "gangnam styled" of the 1960s.

My late father passed on a year after the birth of my daughter, and with that passing, I lost my musical soul mate who had returned home to be with the source. At that time my notion of death was somewhat devastating. Death as we know is an eventuality for everyone but we always never ever discussed it openly and we choose to put it aside far from normal conversation. However the reality is that life and death is as certain as day turns to night, and one day we all will return home to our origin, as a cycle and should not be feared at all. When the soul leaves the body, death occurs as we label it. The body returns to dust but the soul which is eternal lives on. Well said but far from the truth for many of us are lacking in total understanding and acceptance. We tend to keep death at bay with a 100 yard pole. Why is that so?

In our lives we plan for almost everything, from birthdays, anniversaries, graduations, marriages and other celebratory events. We look forward to planning these events with a lot of joy and passion. But no one plans the event of death, which is destined to take place sometime in the future after the day we came to this planet. Because perhaps death is seen as a taboo, no one talks about it. Death is looked upon as a separation, from the physical realm, and because we attach to the physical nature of things with such intensity, no wonder we never want to leave it. I have even heard people say that they have made a pact with GOD so they will live forever. This is an illusion and wishful thinking. But there has been a shift lately in preparing for death. Many people are drawing up their last will and testament, buying up real estate where they can rest in peace. The question then remain, "do we know how to die?" We need to learn how to die and then we begin to live.

To quote a saying "that which was never born will never die". If we see ourselves as a soul that was already in existence eons ago, and today resides temporarily in our physical human body, the soul was really never born. It just transformed from nothingness to form. So when we no longer have a physical body, the soul returns back to where it came from, which is nothingness. The soul was in transition, and was never really born on this planet and thus can never die. It was formless to begin with.

There is however a need to "kill" our current appetites (greed) for wealth, high level positions, status, territorial rights, which stems from our EGO conscious way of living and wanting more. We will come back to this topic a little later.

In early 2001, I was given an opportunity to work out of town and for the first time in 25 years of work career, I had to be away from my family, which was a tough move. I landed in a little town in Malacca, 150 km from central KL, and a 2 hour drive away. Although the distance was not prohibitive, a daily run was not good for the heart. So I stayed out of town from Monday till Friday. Being alone was a difficult period initially but I soon found solace in an apartment overlooking the seafront. This was a bonus view indeed and was one of the conditions given when my wife chose the location. In those initial couple of years I started to pick up the reading habit as I had time on my hands and was drawn towards new age wisdom books. As a reborn and a ready student, many teachers appeared in various encounters and books and for this I am truly blessed to have been guided by these new messages and realizations. This has led to the intriguing question of "what is my purpose here and who am I", really? So why was I given this out of town job, away from family and finding the quiet time to start researching on topics on energy, the unseen realm, laws of attraction and other key universal principles, which today has given me so much more insights to share this journey with you. Indeed there are no coincidences and as I connect the dots, this was definitely planned masterfully by a higher power. Everything that happens in my own experience is for a reason. You have a choice to go with the flow or fight it and experience the consequences later on. Often we do not see the connections but if you trust in the arrangements and follow the path, it will lead to a wonderful outcome eventually.

As we progress through to each of the upcoming stations we will start the fresh phase in this journey to discover the unfolding of our true identity and many new paradigms to be explored. The learning journey will be better experienced if we have a humble attitude to be open to new insights. We need to set aside our preconceived views we have gathered so far in life and allow new dimensions and teachings to be considered. There was a story of a highly learned professor who visited a famous Zen master and said that he wanted to learn the ways of Zen. The professor had introduced himself from a prestigious university with his vast years of educational experience, accomplishments and also his highly acclaimed qualifications. He was cordially invited in and was offered a cup of tea. The Zen master poured the tea and when the cup was full he continued pouring and the tea was spilling over. To his amazement the professor eagerly pointed out and remarked that the tea is overflowing, and the Zen master replied that when one comes with his mind filled up there can be no more teachings to give. Unless you empty your cup only then can we start to pour new tea in for you to taste. Otherwise all new learning will be wasted and will overflow. On the analogy of humility one must lower oneself just like the cup has to be below the level of the teapot in order to receive the tea. If you are arrogant and choose to place the cup above the teapot, when it is poured the tea will just spill on to the floor. Lowering the cup is lowering oneself with the greatest of humility. So for you to have new experiences, be open and have a heart of humility to take in the wisdom. Allow one-self to be open, pour out the old tea and allow you to taste the new brew.

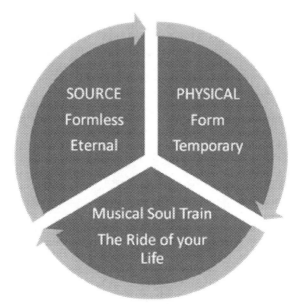

SOURCE
Formless
Eternal

PHYSICAL
Form
Temporary

Musical Soul Train
The Ride of your
Life

Station 2: Who am I

Quote:

*I came from no-where to now-here and
will eventually return to no-where*

Who am I?

Learning from one of my favorite wisdom master, Dr. Wayne Dyer, he teaches us that we came from no-where, to now-here and will return to no-where. This simple one liner struck a cord with me. Yes, we came from NO-WHERE, which is from a non-form existence to form (the physical human we are), when we were conceived in our mothers' womb and later being born into the world. The "soul" resides just after six weeks of conception, and this "invisible" seed can only come from the divine, a plane of higher wisdom that we may not be able to comprehend. When we are born, we are endowed with a divinity of the highest realm. We come from an energy field which is formless and yet has the power of the highest order of creation. At conception and eventual birth we are NOW-HERE. Notice the same letters used but a slight shift of one letter. Is it a mere coincidence or by design? We came from NO-WHERE to NOW-HERE. Close your eyes and soak this in for a moment.

I have now left Station 1 where I had experienced all the physical aspects of living, somewhat domesticated from the teachings and advice from my younger days, to enjoying my youth, starting a work career, and later a family and working my way up the corporate ladder the last 40 years. At this point I am satisfied that I had come a long way and had made good living, but the BIG question still comes to mind—what more is there? This next station is an exciting one that shows me beyond what I know only as my physical domain. There must be something more to this physical equation that meets the eye. There is possibly something more than what my 5 senses tell me. So was I ready to discover beyond? How real is that?

Dr. Dyer in one of his classic book reading called "The Shift", made it clear that we come from a source, and even before conception we already existed but as non form (energy). Upon conception we took on a form smaller than the size of a pin head, and the journey towards planet earth began. And then the drama starts from the day we were born, with what is known as the human domestication process.

The domestication of the human

I was brought up to see myself as the name given by my parents, lived a good 26 years as a son (to my parents) and as a brother (to my sister), and an uncle (to my niece) before I took on a new role of a husband and soon after as a father. To my three children I was also referred to by different naming conventions. My eldest son called me "Pa", my second child, a daughter called me "Dee", and my youngest son referred to me as "Dad". So there I was and with no coincidence in the making, I was "Pa-Dee-Dad" to my three kids, which resembles my forte as a "PARTY-DAD". So here I stand, a single minded person, with multiple reference names, but still the same one and only me. When I joined the workplace, my father reminded me that I should use my surname, my family name, so I was known as Moey Sam Fook, SF Moey, Sam or just Moey. My house name was Philip, known only to family and close friends. So those first 30 years I was attached to these naming conventions, which I later realized that these were just various roles I was playing. I was a son, father, a husband, a brother, a friend, manager, a workmate and so on. I am one and the same person but the reference to others is of a different connection altogether. This analogy is similar to the source spirit, the mother of all creation, and we can call it in whatever reference we have been culturally brought up to believe. For me it has the same oneness. Although many names but from one source.

As a personal reflection, I too, perhaps, came from a higher place, but beyond our limited human comprehension. What we do not see does not necessarily mean it is not there. No one can see gravity but it exists. Some may doubt this higher power but I will pose this question for the imagination. What is it that transpired in your mother's womb from conception that eventually developed a human complete with 60 trillion cells, each with its own unique characteristics and yet aligned to one another so as to become a whole person, fully functioning as one of the highest creations of the modern age? Can ever a human being with its highest of technologies ever do this? The references made to this unknown, the unseen realm are indeed many.

There are many names, such as divinity, universal wisdom, the big bang, the source, the truth, the LIGHT, the TAO and some even say God. I have come to realize that no matter what we label this "invisible" force, it has to be of some wondrous intelligence, of infinite wisdom and ever expanding nature filled with creativity, love, abundance and accepting all of life with grace. How else could I explain the creation of so many manifestations before my very eyes, that I had taken for granted ever so often. The greatest minds of the world have not been able to make a simple rice grain or invent a human eye lash. The truth is there whether we choose to believe it or not. Just as the sun rises each morning, as intended and has no favorite where its rays fall to the earth. As long as we choose to, we can bathe in the sunshine of life, unless we want to remain in the shadows and its darkness. The sun does not care. It is us who make the difference. It is our choosing. Take it or leave it, but do not blame the sun. We can learn so much from nature, which is always giving of itself. Take a simple flower. When in full bloom it beautifies the environment and has a beautiful fragrance, and when it fades off it returns to the earth and fertilizes the ground for the benefit of other plants. It is always of a giving nature.

Contrastingly, we humans are the opposite with a "give me" attitude and the makings of a self centered society, wanting always more, never enough and having a scarcity mindset that stops us from sharing and giving. We operate from a lack of operative thinking, not ever having enough and forever wanting more. As long as we are cared for and our needs are satisfied first, others are considered secondary.

The other fascinating viewpoint is that we are taught to perceive this "invisible" spiritual force outside of ourselves. In Sunday school I was made to picture a wise bearded man in white robes. As I am exposed to further readings today I am slowly opening my own perception of this higher power. I do not have clear examples to prove anything but just to leave you with the thought of your own inner self. Is it possible that you are part of this higher power and divinity, for the simple reason your heart beats automatically and all cells function independently without you barking out any orders. In other words when you do nothing, everything gets done for you. Now I can see the gleam in your eyes to say I therefore am able to stop doing what I am doing, stop working, stop studying and everything gets done for me. Well it is not meant to be that simplistic. There is a combination of human effort and higher power for things to work out. As the bible shares with us, God helps those who help themselves. I can only infer that we need to do our part. This connection from within us to a higher power can best be explained as a cord connection and we need to keep this cord clean. I believe we all have this cord but for some the cord has been contaminated or spread very thin because we have drifted further away by our selfish actions and ways contrary to universal principles. We were all born with the same affinity to this great source but our daily actions have had its consequences. So we need to cleanse and revive this cord to be of a more pristine condition, so that our bandwidth to God is not only clean but fast as well, and is greater than 100MB, and free of charge. So when you are able to connect you will be able to think as what God thinks and be a person with a divine character. And what is God's character and thinking anyway? Does God have a plan for us? Are we a part of his plan? Ever thought of that?

This new paradigm was like a "light bulb" insight for me. What I had always thought as an external source that I had to search for and connect with, there is now a possibility that this source is actually already in me and all I had to do was tune my frequencies to tap into this divine broadband. Then the question arises on how did I begun to tune in to this amazing channel. I have heard of certain practices that they can open a channel to tap into this unseen realm, but was also warned to be careful because this highway is a dual sword. Both light and dark energies can link up to this spiritual highway. I believe you must have a higher level of awareness and be selfless in your thoughts and actions to continue to stay on the right side of things. Is it no different from staying with our values such as honesty, integrity and be of service to others beyond thy self.

Ever wondered how many times when something seems to go wrong, at least that is how we label it, we blame it on something or someone. We choose to see the world through one set of eyes, a one track view only, but do not take a different perspective. These perceptions are hard wired views in our brain, through a sub-conscious level that draws on old memories, and connects itself to the current reality. Dr. Dyer in his magnificent writings of "Change Your Thoughts and You Can Change the World", offers a glimpse of hope to be free of the trappings of the 10,000 things of the world. Neuroscience research now tells us that part of our central brain, called the limbic system is hard-wired from learnt memories and stores all our baggage of the past. That baggage stores our fears, hatred, jealousy, anger, sometimes joy from happy events. It is proven that the human brain scans the environment for threats as an automatic response, so when there is a first meeting of two persons or when you visit a place for the first time, there is an automatic guarded response. In other words the trust level has yet to be established. These emotions drive our behavior and because it has such a strong pull it disengages us from experiencing the present moment. We are always driven to the drama that enfolds from the recalling of memories which are all in the past, and the past is one that we can never change, yet we spent a lot of efforts mulling over it. The next opportunity you have in an interaction of such, please attempt to observe these behaviors. Watch how people justify their actions as a guarded response when something does not produce intended results. No one likes to be labeled as inferior or inefficient. It is an interesting observation. It is a guarded response, which stems from fear. Now perhaps you can appreciate why trust takes time to build and can be destroyed with one act of mistrust.

Where did it go wrong for us?

Adults literally killed our internal music as we were growing up but they had no clue they did it. This internal music was playing as we were children and we were always in the moment of things. Children have little notion of the past and the future. They only focus on what is in front of them this very moment. They can be joyful one moment or cry unashamed at the next instant. They allow their feelings to manifest. As we grow we controlled our feelings for fear of showing our true emotions. We bottle it up inside. Adults however seemed to always know best and what is right for us as we were growing because they felt compelled to do so. This is a fallacy. They will teach us what their own parents taught them. Same old formula, but was done with the best of intentions. We should not blame them as they did not know any better. Unknowingly, our childhood playfulness and innocence was severely suppressed and the child in us virtually died. However, not all is lost, if we know how to revive the song inside us.

To appreciate this gap, watch closely how children play. No judgments, no race card, no qualms that others looked different. In fact they never noticed such differences. They were in a magical world, filled with moment to moment presence. No baggage and no worries of what lies ahead. They were playing their song, filled with magical notes on the stage of life.

As children we lived life to the fullest. We had no inhibitions then to express how we felt. We played when we felt like it, then we stopped to eat and cried when we wanted some attention or we belt it out somewhere else. We did what our hearts told us to do. Those were carefree days, un-doctored and natural. Children are very present in the moment. They are focused on the "now".

Then we started to grow up and we were taught by our well meaning parents, teachers and other folks who caught our attention and started to educate us. Such "education" started us on the road to sadness and drama. Adults started hooking our attention and we were told to study hard, find a good job, get married, raise kids and then retire into the sunset. All well and good except that we had baggage of sadness and fear engrained in us. The child in us was suppressed and we never went there again at all. The inner child has been neglected for so long. There is always a child in us. Just imagine our happiest moments, when we can do silly things in safe setting, in a party playing games, on the beach just laying around, or at a mamak (local food) stall chilling out with friends.

We also grew up looking for rewards and avoided punishments. The name of the game was to do something to maximize rewards and minimize the risks. Thus we were fearful of trying out new things, new ventures for fear of failure due to uncertainty. The feelings were based on external factors that we seek to validate our actions and our happiness and sadness came from these external forces, namely by opinions and acceptance. We were happy when someone praised us, but that same person can condemn you the next day, and you are then saddened. We were paralyzed by opinions of others. We looked for acceptance from others and their rewards and we lapped this up each time. We feared if we did not live up to another's expectations, we are subject to verbal reprimand and we could be devastated. Another act of domestication was to have an EGO. The EGO—which means "Edging God Out", becomes the downfall of many, because we placed too much emphasis on wanting to be right, having the last word in, and drama starts when you are in the EGO mode which attracts trouble.

EGO taught us that we become who we are through what we own (money, property, and cars), our official position (titles), and what others thought about us (their opinions). Little did we know that all these were external validations and as good as it is to have them, these can be taken away in one instant. So we can shift from being happy to sadness in a jiffy. When we rely on external factors to make us happy, we become a victim to the whims and fancies of others. This is dangerous territory to tread.

EGO also taught us to win every conversation because we could display our intelligence. Attending the top schools made us more important compared to others. While I do not downplay the essence of wealth from these associations, we have to check our EGO very so often. EGO teaches us that we can be better than others, but GOD living teaches us we can only be better than whom we were before. We are not here to change others, but to change ourselves. The idea that we can change another person is wishful thinking.

In a nutshell, the process of domestication and seeing the world as the survival of the toughest has created a thinking that requires us to win all battles, sometimes at all costs. We live from a scarcity mindset that sharing means lesser for us, and we must take what is rightly ours. We expect to be paid for all work we do, and the amount we make shows how successful and important we have become. This is the world on the physical level. Sadly this is the only world many know. All the learnt behaviors are stored in our central brain system (limbic system), and automatically fires up when we encounter a situation that is either a threat or a reward state. Some writings refer to this as the subconscious mind or an inner child that is neglected, and believe this is the source of our drama unfolding everyday, and unless these old memories are "cleaned" there is no freedom from the past, and a blindside to the path of happiness.

To appreciate further how we evolved to where we are today we need to go back to look at the ages of civilization starting with the age of the hunter/gatherer. That age focused very much on the individual and his own power. He alone was responsible for feeding himself and his family. He mastered hunting skills which was fundamental to being "successful". The self became the center of the universe. He survived because of his own hunting and survival skills and physical prowess. Today we cannot survive on this mode, but how did we evolve? We are now approaching the third station to uncover what lies there to teach us even more. Allow your minds to be bathed in newer dimensions without expectations. That is the best way to enjoy and take in the moment, and perhaps learn a thing or two.

Station 3: Wisdom of the Ages

Quote:

When you cannot change others, you must then be the change you desire to see in the world

The Wisdom of the Ages

If you ever studied the ages of civilization there are in fact five distinct levels, starting from the beginning of time of the **hunter/gatherer** whose primal goal was to hunt food to feed him-self and his family on a day to day basis. He had no refrigerators to store his food so it was not wise to kill more than he could consume. Everyday was a new challenge to put food on the table. That was his living mode. I believe in those early days there was a deep connection with nature as a provider and the hunters only took what was needed. There was no need for accumulations like what we experience in the so called modern society today. The early hunters and gatherers were one with nature and one with their source of being. They had that knowing, and their connection with nature. The "I" was of primary importance. He relied solely on his own steam (a single individual).

Then we had the next civilization shift, which was the **age of agriculture**. The mindset shift was no more of the former thinking of a single individual and getting instant results, but to embrace a concept to plant seeds that could yield a harvest 50 to 500 times more than what a hunter could achieve. The difference did also lie in the fact that you had to allow the period of harvest to complete the cycle. The nurturing cycle was required before any output was achieved. So from a singular product (in the hunter gatherer age) came the concept of mass production. Man had progressed significantly with the idea of duplication. This new concept can never be appreciated if you had stayed on the mindset level of a hunter/gatherer. He will never understand the concept of the law of harvest since he always had his food at the instant he had hunted down an animal. To plant a seed and wait for weeks was inconceivable for him. Man had to change his way of thinking and so he did, eventually.

The next phase was the **age of industrialization**, started in early 1900s. Factories were the mainstay of this age. The production capabilities grew even 100 times more than that of agricultural age, although we know that many modern farms today do use mechanized equipment to manage thousands of acres. In terms of managing people, the industrialized age focused on the top boss to lead the way. He was seen as the sole "thinker" of the organization and everyone else was just the "hands" and "backs". Workers were hired to follow orders, and not paid to think. They had little to no voice in the human endeavor. Ever wondered why unions started sprouting then. It was to create a voice of the people, for the people. The human spirit was heavily suppressed in the masses that filled the factory floor. Those first industrial days, people were hired for their manual efforts (literally hands and backs). No one was interested in their thinking, after all, the thinking was the sole right of the top boss. No one would ever ask a lowly paid person what he thought. As seen in modern management today we see more organizations engaging their workforce with employee work circles and team based environments. From the 1960s management began to realize that each worker had a brain and they could think and had even more knowledge than anyone else about his own workplace. The human spirit started to be recognized and was to soar to greater heights. Industrial best practices started with self directed work teams (SDWT) and employee involvement teams (EIT). More autonomy was given to the workforce. This new phase did not go down well with some managers, who still had the old industrialized age mindset. I believe this to possibly be a self preservation response to not letting go of command and power.

Today we see a great shift towards the **information age**. Industrialization remains the backbone in modern day business, and the advent of higher computing power and vast communication networks have made yet another leap forward. The world is indeed smaller with the vast connections at speeds never experienced before. The first computers needed a room to house it and by the same comparison this same computing power can be held in your hand today. Information is now at our finger-tips thanks to Mr. Google and his lot. Imagine if you still had the industrialized age mentality to manage your people, and tell them to follow your instructions and not question them. It will be chaotic, because now they have a reference source to validate your views. Today the study of Gen Y has become a widespread topic in the field of modern management. Managing Gen Y is no more an option. It has become a necessity because these are your current resources going forward. While we are still bathing warmly in the age of electronics, gadgets and latest gizmos, I feel we have also lost the human touch in many ways. Just observe today how many people sitting next to each other would rather have intense eye contact with their mobile devices than connect with the human being sitting next to them. Even families do this. Ever wondered why there are communication breakdowns between spouses, children and workmates. This is because we have lost the art of communicating with each other at a deeper emotional level. How sad this has become! So you need to ponder that yes, on one hand we have progressed from the days of the hunter/gatherer to the modern enterprise and high tech gizmos, and yet the human spirit has not been fully engaged. Something is sadly missing.

In the midst of all this modernized chaos, an emerging force is being felt today. In the last 20 years or so there is a movement back to the past (more of returning to where we started). This means that we are slowly but surely been pulled back to the beginning of time, where it all started with the tenets of love and wisdom. The world is changing before our eyes. We see unprecedented events all around us, many are hugely devastating events. We hear of those preparing survival packs, building underground shelters, and preparing for a worst turn of worldly events. We have seen earthquakes, forest fires and tsunami. Ever wondered why we are at this crossroad at a time when it appears that modern science is at its peak? Can't we do something about all this? What do you think?

Surely with our latest technologies and greatest of minds we can surpass these events. We have the largest computers ever, the fastest, the tallest, the biggest of everything in the last 200 years of human endeavor. Can't we handle this? When nature unleashes its power, great cities just fall to their knees. Great winds, rain and typhoons have been felt in recent times. Forest fires and floods come in rapid succession. Why do you think that is so? There is a possible reason to the changing tides and weather conditions.

There have been great strides in material development for the last 150 years and today we enjoy the modernization and vast communication networks that span the globe and into outer space. The age of materialism is at the turning point and humans have placed too much emphasis on the pursuit of materials and its further accumulation. We are at an impasse point and need to play down our materialistic demands. We need to return to times of our origin and be more God conscious in our actions. We have perhaps come towards a full circle and the **age of wisdom** is upon us today. There are signs and messages out there which we need to pay attention to because these are times of change urgently needed before it is too late.

I can only say we must accept the fact that a higher wisdom exists and all that is happening is for a reason. I do not profess to have all the answers but we must continue to search deep within us for the ultimate understanding of such events. It has to be a deep realization that we need to achieve "satori" (closing the gap) between us and the source (God). The further apart we are, the greater the need to experience compensation phenomena. This new thinking has to evolve and it is the time to embrace the age of wisdom and return to the tenets of divine principles as our final saving grace for humanity. This wisdom is beyond normal human intelligence, and it requires a new acceptance that we no longer have control and we are doomed if we continue on the path of materialism, destroying the planet with deforestation, polluting our seas and killing our animals to the point of extinction and toxic waste discharge from industrialization, excessive use of chemicals in agriculture, doctoring livestock and fruits for larger profits and the list goes on. Even the global economies are being seriously challenged and many are spiraling downwards with fiscal cliffs and what have you.

When the student is ready—opening up to new dimensions

I have always believed that when the student is ready the teacher will appear. Well, for me personally, the last 10 years spent in pleasant isolation somewhere working out of town, I had much quiet time in the early mornings and started the reading habit and re-booted my student mode. Yes I was looking for meaning and purpose in my life and generally what life is all about. I already had much to be thankful for but I knew deep inside there was more to learn and to comprehend. And lo and behold the wisdom teachers started to come into my life. When you are tuned in to a path you wish to travel, somehow people and things appear before you. In the past they seemed to elude you, and I now know that what you think about is what you become. As we tune our mind frequencies the universe responds in kind and by some unexplainable fact, they just show up. Your life changes by the people you meet and the books that you read, so here I would like to share some of the greater teachings and concepts that have made me a better person than I was before. The process has allowed me to have a deeper realization of who I am and where I came from and my purpose here. Each view is reproduced from my own reflections and it complements one another for the total transformational process, and allows a larger picture to be formed in the final analysis. I owe a debt of gratitude to all those who have taught me and continue to show me every day the new possibilities as long as I am open to it.

The student/teacher relationship is like a tango dance, as it takes two to tango as is commonly said. You do not know who the leader is as the role switches automatically. In everything that we do we are the student and the teacher at the same time. As a parent you begin to teach your child the ways of the world and in turn your child teaches you the innocence and joyfulness in the moment. The lessons each impart are different and if we understand this basic principle we are always open to new learning. That is how I have taken the position as I have grown a little older. Ask me 25 years before and I would have probably given a different perspective. I once heard that as you get older you start having hope for others and want more for them than yourself, and perhaps that is true for me, and this is to be my "teacher legacy" that I would leave for those who want to become a student once more. After all as we teach we begin to learn even more. When we take the position of a student we humble ourselves to ride on the teacher's ability to impart knowledge and wisdom to us. Watching a child play can teach you a lot if you are observant and see the "teacher" in them. What message are they imparting to you? If you take on this new paradigm everything out there is waiting to teach you more and as a student you catch that wisdom which in turn allows you to be in a better position to impart it to someone else when it is your role to teach. It is an evolving cycle. I encourage you to consider this viewpoint as you change the way you look at things and the things you look at will change right before your very eyes.

Beyond ordinary human awareness

I talked about the power of domestication in the early chapters, and understanding this process has allowed me to appreciate others much better. Because we come from different backgrounds and cultures and knowing that no two minds are alike, we need to respect each other's view of the world. Each person's paradigm is very real to him or her and that is how they respond to the world around them. We fundamentally act from two basic emotional levels, which is either from an act of love or a response stemming from fear. In many cases it is driven from the latter. When we develop more understanding why people behave the way they do, we reach a higher level of awareness that helps us navigate the daily events more effectively. We do not get emotionally involved because what people say and do is never about you. It is ultimately about how they feel they need to react to the world that surrounds them. Their actions validate their need to be that person they project themselves to be. Examples are: I am a manager so I need to be tough and decisive otherwise my bosses think I am weak. I am a parent and I can do no wrong so my children should listen to me. I am a teacher so my students should listen to me. I am a trained engineer so do not question my recommendations on the production floor. You sort of get what I am slowly alluding to and we see this ever so often in many circumstances and conversations.

This had made me realize that each person have their own degree of fear (subconsciously) that have been built up and accumulated over the years, and the words spoken and actions taken are an exact reflection of their view of the world and how they choose to respond to it. When you have an urge to control everything you cannot let go. The fear of losing control causes you to micro manage and need to know everything. Many people micro manage and find this comforting, and are blind sided to the negative implications it has on others. When one is problem-focused, and looking for blame and excuses, you will find it, no question, and it is never easy to look forward with an alternate view. In my career over the last 40 years, I have dealt with auditors, bless their souls. In an audit environment the natural domestication is to look for potential faults, fraud possibilities and largely focusing on what can people or system do and possibly go wrong. Why, because that is how they were trained. When they focus on this approach, that is what the mind congregates towards and although I am grateful that they point out certain weaknesses as preventive measures, the focus paradigm is obvious. On a balanced note when I ask them what would be one good practice they saw in their review work, they are speechless. Simply because they were looking for faults and they never noticed what people did right. I believe what you look for you will eventually find, and you are blind-sided to everything else. They are fundamentally good people, and it is the mindset they take based on the perceived job that they undertake, and the domestication of the profession. How can this change? Simple, change your thoughts and the world around you changes too. So when a new wiring is established to look at both sides of the coin then their view differs and they see a new perspective. Ever had the experience that when you finally decided to buy a particular car model and you have made a down payment, suddenly you see the same model everywhere. That is because your brain has tuned in to the image and scans the environment looking for similar associations. Fascinating, but true! It has happened to me time and again. I thought these were coincidences but I know better today.

In the study of management and on the topic of how most leaders function, there is a frequent tendency that many prefer to tell and seldom ask for solutions. Telling seems easier when you think you know everything, and have all the answers and appear smarter than most. This approach is quite normal after all you are more senior and have had many more years of experience under your belt. This is both EGO consciousness at play as well as fear of letting go of control, or appearing inferior by not knowing everything. Telling others what to do and problem focused views seemed to be what many supervisors and managers gravitate to. They often take the position of power and have a "know it all" attitude. It is little surprising why the human spirit in their staff members never seem to rise up to the occasion. They are simply not given that opportunity to speak up or to make recommendations and were never asked. Worst off, they will even talk down on their staff. The fallacy that all leaders must know everything and it is a taboo to ask for help, as it shows weakness to the lower ranks. We find this in the way emperors and conquerors ruled the world in the early days. The great warlords ruled over others by instilling fear, as anyone who went against their authority was instantly beheaded. This act of aggression is steeped in history and sadly it is still practised today in so called modern society, from the advent of the age of industrialization. Thus the perceived act of obedience is stemmed from the basic emotion of fear. How wonderful if these acts could actually stem from love. The world would become an eternal garden of "eden" once more.

On the other side of the spectrum, when we engage with such superiors or others who seem to know much more than you, you have to understand where they operate from. Most often, it is from a platform of fear of losing control and fear of letting go of power. They see a need to set very tight boundaries which will narrow the talents of others to be displayed, as these will always be suppressed. Instead of being negative to these persons we should take on a new paradigm. When we understand such tendencies in how others behave and react to situations, we need to stop taking it personally. In the study of **The 4 Agreements**, which is a Toltec wisdom teaching on how to be truly free and happy, it teaches us that what others say and do is never about you. It is about their perceived view of the world, which is their reality, and based on their own domestication process. If we accept all opinions personally we allow the "poison arrows" to penetrate us. In the end we not only feel the negative energy coming towards us but we also allow ourselves to be the inner victim of such abuse. So practise not taking anything personally. It does not matter if we are getting positive comments or otherwise we need to find our own middle road which is a platform of peace. We always place a label on everything as good or bad. We are elated when good events happen and sadness for the opposite, not realizing these are external conditions and we place our emotions on it. In reality it is what it is. Once you are able to appreciate this new view, and learn its principles, it will free you from the emotional roller coaster. When you change the way you look at things, the things you look at will change. For me this is the same as taking the middle road, staying center to your core energy and not be swayed either way. The great teachers all possess this trait of inner strength and wisdom and calm serenity. In Steven Covey's teachings he refers to this as principle centered behavior.

Mastery of love

Using the metaphor of an orange, when you squeeze one, what comes out? The answer is of course, orange juice. Never will apple juice come out of an orange. The answer is simply because that is "what is inside". Nature makes no mistakes. Never will you get apple juice from an orange.

Now let us squeeze you, by making a bad remark on you or someone challenges you in the workplace, or a car overtakes you on the wrong lane. What comes out from you will likely be "foul" language. Such manifestation is no surprise because you have all these in you. Out of you comes anger, frustration, jealously and other negative vibrations when your hot buttons are pushed. Many of these emotions are from ego based consciousness and we cannot stand others being above us or making us look small. So if you were an "orange" and we squeeze you, out comes from you foul smelling pus! Therefore we all need to return to the original essence of purity and restore the pure "orange" juice in us. That is the goal.

When a sage is asked why they always bestow love and harmony to all they meet, in their actions and also in their words, it is simply because that is all they have. That is all that is in them and they know no other way to act. We too have that capability to love but we choose to store the negatives as well. It is important that we be mindful of such tendencies and instead attempt to practise to be in a state of gratitude each and every day. To be able to do this we have to start from within. How can we give something that we do not have? When we learn to love and appreciate ourselves, only then can we have the capacity to love others. Love transcends all because it is no more seeing the world as our competition, our shortages and our scarcity mindset. It is only when you realize your purpose and know about loving humanity you are able to do for others more than what you do for yourself. This does not mean you become a lesser person. In essence you become a bigger one and are not intimidated by EGO or wanting to look good in the eyes of others. You know your self worth and knowing the highest divinity that is within you, and not dependent on the material extremities of the physical world. When you see others as also a divine creation as with all of nature you become one with God and his children. Irrespective what others think of you, it has little consequence when you are inspired (in spirit) to do work that is God consciousness and not from EGO consciousness.

Hence the mastery of love is the ultimate wisdom to attain when we are fully in awareness of our domestication legacy and begin to transform our thinking to a higher plane.

Appreciating the power of silence

In school we are taught to read, write and speak. We are never really taught how to listen. In a conversation, we do not know how to listen effectively. By keeping silent and listening intently allows us to feel the other person and show them that we care. Effective listening skills are not commonly practised. We prefer to lay out our version of our thoughts to others. We do not connect deeply as we fail to seek first to understand. Learn to be silent. Stop wanting to answer based on your own paradigm. Everyone needs to listen more and talk less. Ever wondered why we were born with two ears and only one mouth. God gave us these simple signs which we have ignored all this while.

The great sage Lao Tzu taught us to be "Living in Calmness". We have a choice to react when we are in turmoil or face events driven by external forces. We can be joyful and exhilarated one moment and then down in the dumps as if the world has fallen apart around us the next moment. The analogy is like being swayed by the winds of circumstances and if our roots are weak, we will be destroyed. Our roots have to be firm and strong which is our choice to be. Choose stillness and calmness as a base for your feeling tone because this is the WAY of being. Feel this presence in the early hours of the morning before the world wakes up and goes into a frenzy with the workings of the 10,000 things coming to life. In the teachings of Buddha, we are all told to always take the middle path. My reflection on this is similar to being still (calm), in both joyous times and sad times. By another paradigm, good and bad are just labels we give to a situation. If we like it we label it good, and vice versa. There are no good and no bad. We have been molded to label opposites to everything. Tall and short, thin and fat, young and old, small and big and the list go on. Whatever happens is designed to be. It is what it is, so learn to be still and accept the circumstance and move on. These are the secret pathways to grow your roots to be on firmer ground. You have the ability to do this practice, and it is a matter of choice to be firstly aware and then find that sanctuary of learning.

The power of silence is also apparent and fundamental when you write music. Without the "space" in between each of the notes, there will be literally no music. Without the pause in between each note, we will only hear one continuous sound that has no meaning. In the busy world we live in, we need to take a time out (and find that space) to get re-energized before the next step. I once encountered a gentleman who practised keeping silent for 24 hours. Just try to stop talking for an hour and feel the difference. We each have to find our own space, to find out who we really are and what do we stand for. Today we all live in a rush society and we go about getting things done, seemingly very busy. We can't even sit for a moment at home without turning the cable TV on. We bombard our minds with so much information and events that we numb ourselves without knowing it. We become a slave to the square box in our living rooms. Ever seen people who are like that? Anyone you know. Are you like that? If so make a change today and see what it can do for you. Take time to have some quiet time.

It is said, the truly wise speaks little and when he does we need to sit up and soak in every spoken word. Those who speak the most and sometimes loud offer little to anyone. They speak so loud that "we can hardly hear a word they are saying" is a common phrase we hear.

I had a pleasant experience attending the marriage of one of my close friend's daughter who has a hearing impaired condition and I was fascinated at the event that took place, with 70% of the reception who were hearing impaired. We have been conditioned to view them as handicapped and wonder how they would function in society. At that reception we felt we were the odd ones as we had no clue what was transpiring. Within their own community of friends of similar condition I could see no such indications of the impairment and the wedding was conducted smoothly and beautifully. There was even a musical performance using non verbal communication and it was a beautiful sight to behold. I could see joy in their faces and they were living life. I could see the sparkle in their eyes when we greeted each other as no words were spoken. It was my first encounter attending such an event and it was an eye opener. Perhaps I was the one who was "handicapped" to make such judgments in the first place. Within the silence there was heart and soul and again this enforces the power of toning it down. Speaking less and hearing more. The world needs this more so in today's environment of conflict and ego based conversations and negotiations. You open up the morning paper and you see the reporting of many people in positions of power saying things which would have best been kept silent. This is followed by others who will rebut their views and is a never ending story line.

I have also come across the teachings of other great wisdom teachers and here I will share two which have helped me in my quest towards happiness. These teachings were introduced to me in my search for greater knowledge and spiritual connectivity. One is called **The WORK** by Byron Katie and the **Power of NOW** by Ekhart Tolle. Below is a short synopsis of each and if you are interested to know more please read the book itself.

The Work—what is the reality?

I came across THE WORK by Byron Katie and she taught the concept of not expecting anything from others. When you demand of others to change to your personal wants and expectations, you are truly in a false illusion. If you say "I wish my son would obey my instructions", you are creating an illusion in that way of thinking. By asking the question of how do you know it is absolutely true, and then say "what would your feelings be if you did not make those expectations". The answer is that we will be free. When we believe that people should react to our expectations, it is a sure recipe to fail. No one owes you anything to change, but you have the power to change the way you look at things, and when you do, then a new paradigm of thinking is formed. Not only do you pose the questions of truth but the turnaround is important. So instead of saying "my son should listen to me more", the turnaround is that perhaps "I should also listen to my son more". And when you stop having this desire to have your son listen to you, you will also be free of human expectation otherwise this nagging thought will stay and haunt you. The Work teaches you not to judge, even yourself, and the premise is that the wisdom you seek is within you. This is validated by another wisdom teaching that says change is up to us, because for things to change, we have to change first. Change is constant and we are the best agent of our own character development. For greater appreciation please read the book The Work.

The Power of NOW

The past, present and future holds 3 distinct reference points for many of us. When something happens, especially sad or hurtful events, we have a tendency to cling on to the events. Our mind experiences the event modes, hardwires it and stores it in the sub-conscious mind, and if we keep recalling the event it becomes your current reality. The recollection of past events does not help anyone. Bringing back old memories are like playing an old record time and again. When we become obsessed with the past we cannot move forward. The opposite of thinking of the future is also another point of discussion. What you now attempt to experience on a future event is insane because the future does not exist today.

The only point in time that really matters is NOW. It is this very present moment that is relevant because you are here. You do not know what will happen an hour from now and you can never change what happened an hour ago. So begin to live at the present moment because it will never come again. Often we get through one event to reach a destination. We prepare for a trip and use the journey as a means to reach a destination, and we actually forget to appreciate and enjoy the journey itself. Forget about enjoying life after you retire, enjoy life today as you work towards your retirement. Otherwise you miss a big part of the experience.

So as the soul train moves on let us bask in the present moment at each of the stations of life. When we surrender to the moment we allow ourselves to be open to so many vibrations surrounding us. As I sit in the early mornings listening to soft music in the background it moves my soul to be calm and this has many a day allowed my feelings to put pen to paper. There is no real thinking, only feeling of what I choose to share. Cherish each moment. With the sounds of birds in the trees and the dawn breaking we are already in heaven. So the reality is here and NOW. The question is whether you have had the chance to discover it. Or are you blocked by the FOG of daily chores and the 10,000 things that Lao Tzu tells us about, that is eagerly waiting for you on the horizon.

The music in you

I have heard of "a cappella", which are songs that are being sung without any accompaniment of instruments. Singers rely solely on their vocal skills, but I have never heard one live. One day my niece bought tickets to a 4 person group from Finland named FORK ROCKCAPPELLA. I have never heard of them and thought to myself that well, this could be an interesting event and I was totally blown away with the two hour show. This leads me to my next upcoming station, to explore how does your music play? Here I saw on stage 4 persons, 2 male and 2 female vocalists who only used their God given vocal chords and they literally blew the audience away. People were up on their chairs and dancing as you would see in a full rock concert, but these quartet had no big amplifiers and sophisticated instruments to help them. The two hour show gave me an insight of what it means to enjoy the moment, to immerse oneself in full presence and be in the zone. When you are able to do that you give 100% of your attention and energy to what you do, where you are, whom you are with. This same intensity can be displayed by just having even a decent conversation with another human being. Try it to taste the "dance of insight", to experience a delightful interaction of souls in a deep and inspired conversation. Many times we avoid such interactions and we rush about so much we have forgotten to look into the eyes of others, as windows to their souls. We fail to take time to make time. We are indeed a rush society. Why? In a book entitled **The Dash**, we see life as being born and we dash to the finish line called death and wondered how life passed us by so quickly and we seem to have accomplished so very little. When I refer to little I do not mean one's self accumulations of wealth and materials, but more of what have you done for others and the legacy you leave behind to be remembered by. Self centered individuals have little capacity to give, in fact, it is far from their vocabulary, and it never entered their minds to be any different. Every man for himself, charity begins at home is interpreted for own benefit. With all their riches, their music within fail to surface, and if not checked, they will die with the music still waiting to be played. A joyful life is in giving. In the prayer of St Francis, one line says, it is in giving to all men that you shall receive. Start with a heart to serve others and be a giver and many miracles will unfold for you.

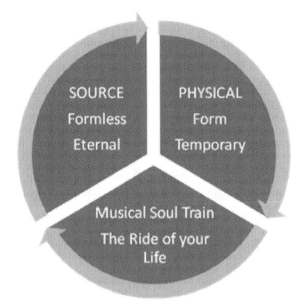

SOURCE
Formless
Eternal

PHYSICAL
Form
Temporary

Musical Soul Train
The Ride of your
Life

Station 4: Is the song still playing

Quote:

Make me a channel of your peace

Is the Song still playing?

We all carry a song inside us. It is the song that makes us human. I deliberately used the term "song" and not music as yet. Although some may feel it as similar and insignificantly different, I believe we all have first to choose a song. That song has to be learnt and practised 100 times until it becomes natural to you. Only when the song is mastered can you begin to make music. It does not matter if you do not play a musical instrument or do not sing or have two left feet when asked to dance. It is not about that ability, but more on what is the rhythm of life that is in you. Music transcends all cultures because it is a universal platform. Take a drum and hit it and after a while our primal instincts comes to being. Try it, start a beat club. You can use a pail and a brush as your instrument. It even sounds better after a while and develops higher momentum when more join in to be in harmony with you. It has a drawing energy.

So what is a song? May I take the liberty to share an example and this may be a possible song choice for you to be sung from within. It is a famous hymn prayer from St Francis of Assisi and is entitled "Make Me a Channel of Your Peace". This prayer tells us that we need to be the channel for change. Here are extracts of the beautiful lyrics:

Make me a channel of your peace.
Where there is hatred let me bring your love

Where there is injury, your pardon, Lord
And where there's doubt, true faith in You.
Where there's despair in life, let me bring hope
Where there is darkness, only light
And where there's sadness, ever joy

It is always easy for us to ask for peace in the world and hope that it comes. Rather than ask for it, become an **instrument of change**. As the prayer guides us, to be a channel for peace, and it starts at home and then your workplace and the community you live in. It only begins with a small step, and we are the only ones who can make it happen. Do not look for others, your spouse, your brother or friends to take that step. You are in control of your actions and only you and you alone make the choice to begin. When there is hatred, make a choice to bring love, where there is darkness be the light for others and where there is doubt share your faith. By being there for others during times of need, holding their hands, or lending a sympathetic ear are the simple actions we can take.

The above hymn prayer guides us to acknowledge that we need not seek a higher power external to ourselves as this power resides within us. Simply because we came from that divine source we can see it in our highest self, which is a connection to our source of being. Thus we can make that change and be the instrument of change, one step at a time. This is an important and key realization (higher awareness). When we ask that we ourselves need to be consoled at times of weakness or trouble, or to be understood and be loved, we need to change our paradigm that we should be the first to console, understand and love others. With love we enter the realm of the high heavens because GOD is love. When we are able to tap into this consciousness we created a high energy pattern that flows towards our very being (remember I mentioned we are born from formless energy to physical form at the point of conception). Then we find the answers in the mystical arrangements that manifest itself beyond our mental capacity.

When this becomes your mantra, your song begins to unfold inside you and once you master it there is music in the air, and it is this music that brings life to all. Every one of us has this song, and it can be anything you choose to be, but please do not keep this song inside you. Some will share their voices or opinions for just causes and this is also a song they sing out loud and clear. When we are united we are capable of great things and when the symphony of the human spirit is on song, we are invincible. The world will stand up and listen to your music. Take the example of Nelson Mandela when he finally ended the apartheid in South Africa and became his country's president after his release from imprisonment, his song was being sung. Look at Au Yang Suu Kyi of Burma and what she has done and fought for in her struggles against the junta is also another fine example of a song being sung at the highest stages of the world. They became the international symbol of peace against the highest form of aggression. We may not be on par with these two examples of great spiritual warriors but we all have our own unique voice that is God given, and is always waiting to be sung.

Some people tell me they have no rhythm. This is absolutely not true, because as long as your heart beats you have rhythm. As long as you can breathe you have a rhythm. If you can walk, you have it too. All it takes is a little coaxing and you have the beat of your life. Close your eyes and feel your heart beat. It goes "dup-dup, dup-dup", and that is rhythm, and very consistent.

Everything around you has a rhythm. Watch a bird in flight, see the sun set, feel the wind in your face. It has its own rhythm. The four seasons has its own rhythm, and each has a unique mystical touch. An effective conversation has a natural rhythmic flow of give and take, looking for solutions, follows a path of thinking, allowing each party to speak and at the same time listening with your heart. Pause and reflection, and then having an insight are again rhythmic in its execution. When it all comes together it is magical and you can feel it. As already mentioned, take the four seasons that come and go as an example of natures' rhythm. The changes blend so that when winter breaks, spring is here, and the transition is magical. Ice melts and little droplets form and are in a pure form. The sun emerges and with the cold passing on, a new air of freshness is felt, and a new dawn comes into being. Just as life moves on, we are constantly changing yet we are connected. Each cell is being replaced just as each cell expires every minute. In spite of all the changes, we need to be in unity and remain whole, because this is the expectation of GOD, in the cycle of birth and re-birth.

Conflict causes you to be off track, off the beat, and off the rhythm. Why, because conflict goes against the fabric of love and it is painful, has low energy and is definitely "off-step" to the harmony of things. There is no music in a conflict, only sadness and a mournful sound in the background. Watch out for the negative energies of your life— worry, jealousy, anger, hatred, fear, which all sound like broken records. Obnoxious people are also energy drainers, so we avoid them. Same goes for self centered people, and you can spot them a mile away. They will only associate with you when there is something for them to benefit from their association with you otherwise it is wasted effort on their part. Do not judge or hate them, but understand their nature because that is how their paradigm of the world is, due largely to their own domestication process to be loud as a demonstration of their need to appear superior to others. They have to be who they are. Opinions need to be said, arguments need to take place but so be it.

In the final analysis do not take anything personally. In the world of music we need to tune our instruments because they get off track when left idle for some time and a poorly tuned instrument sounds like a really bad broken record.

So tuning is necessary, just as we need to recalibrate every time you have an argument or a difference of opinions, to get back in tune, which is your center. As we argue our emotions get the better of us and may say things we regret later, and there is negativity flowing outwards. This foul air generated needs to be cleaned. When we tune our instruments we can use tuning devices, but for a seasoned musician, they only need to use their God given hearing, their ears. So what does the metaphor of tuning an instrument mean for us? I will like to offer the following propositions.

Tuning is basically returning to the center, your core, which means we align back to the basic principles of the universe. Some of these principles I have adopted are to practise stillness in times of turmoil. Close your eyes at that moment and concentrate on your breathing, which gives you life. Be mindful of the air that goes into your lungs and vibrates in your body. Then open your heart and tap into your divinity that is great love. Start to love that greatness that is bestowed upon you. Until you silence your mind and allow the love in your heart to surface, how can you really forgive and send love out into the universe. How can you give love to all that you meet in the pathway of humanity? How can you give something that you yourself do not have? Ponder on this. Therefore everything starts with us. It is never about others, it is always about us. To quote Gandhi, "when you cannot change others, you must then become the change that you intend to be".

For those of you who are musicians, when you integrate yourself with your instrument of choice, beautiful music is produced when you feel the music within your body, and generate your own brand of energy. Playing an instrument requires us to experience a feeling which is beyond just being on a mental level. When you use only the mind, it is a process of playing. When you use the whole body, mind and soul you are immersed with the vibrations from the instrument. When you engage your heart you reach a unique plane of freedom of expression. Each one of us has a unique tone. When others join in, their individual tones blend together just like a full orchestra in unison. This is the tapestry of humanity that although appearing different on the outside we are indeed deeply connected on the inside.

The entire globe has a heart beat. We have a heartbeat. We are connected to this singular rhythm. There is unison between all living things and all of nature. So learn to play the music within. Close your eyes and be ever mindful of your feelings, and be in touch with even the sounds of insects in the night. Listen and hear the humming which portrays nature in its natural state.

Playing music in a group requires the basic skill of leading, listening and following. A jam session is where a group of musicians gather and on an ad hoc basis will make music together and this allows each musician to blend in and sometimes act as a lead and sometimes a follower. The analogy is also applicable when we interact with others. We learn to listen, act and give feedback, which is like a jam session. Know when you are required to lead, but at the same time know when to slide back and listen. Allowing others to lead then gives you a role of follower, a lower seat, which can be humbling. When you can give up your leadership you allow others to play a different role, and you display a greater part of yourself. You subjugate your EGO for the good of the group. Never be selfish but be generous. When you are generous this can become contagious and others will follow. As you give, so you shall also be able to receive. This is a powerful principle to be mindful of. When musicians are able to give and take, a jam session comes alive and it is a natural state of flowing with others. There is no EGO. Each will play their part and together make beautiful and creative music. So it will be similar if a team acts in the same manner, the results shall come forth because of the synergistic power of the team and never on any one individual alone.

Now let us go back temporarily to my music studio, my sanctuary. Every time I visit I look around to see which instrument I need to pick up and play. Sometimes I just go to the conga drums and belt it out, starting slowly with a beat that matches my heart and slowing building up a mood of joy and gratitude. Some musicians I have come across say that you need to live, breathe and play the instrument of choice 24 hours a day to be really good at it. I tend to believe that we first need to live and breathe 24 hours a day, and then play the instrument of choice. Once you can get hold of the art in the joy of living, that joy will transcend into the instrument you embrace and in collaboration, you make beautiful and soulful music. The music that comes out of you tells a thousand words and represents who you really are (your true calling). Be fully alive each day, and sing a song of joy in your hearts. When you can do this it will show in your voice, your body language and your confidence.

I view all my instruments with the same feeling as I relate to my children. Although I own many musical instruments, I can pick up only one at a time. Each instrument is built in a unique manner and no two instruments are alike. I own 3 guitars at the time of writing, and each would have their own feel, sounds and characteristics. I am on purpose to declare that I have 3 guitars at time of writing because more will be adopted into the music room in the near future. How can we put a number on the magical instruments of life?

I relate the above analogy with also the people whom I meet and each meeting has to be a holy encounter. No two persons are alike, even if they are born twins. They are separate souls and even no two brains are alike. This is because we are each a unique being and as we come from the greater source of creation, there is a unique purpose, just like my guitars, each created to make their own unique sounds of music on this planet. When we encounter others, we must see the potential in them and also at the same time acknowledge the divinity that is bestowed in each human being. The word (human being) itself suggests that we are "human" in the physical form and "being" as related to a formless nature. In combination a spiritual presence has been embodied in a temple of the physical body.

The body is similar to the guitar or the piano or any other instrument. It is material and physical in nature. The spark only comes from what is inside the instrument waiting to be played, and unless you use this you will be at an ordinary level of existence. Both the musician and their instrument are capable of creating wonder and the music will wait in silence to be played. It is up to you to crank up this music. Music is the energy that you give out, the vibrancy that stems from one who sees life as one magical journey. It will manifest in your tone of voice, your enthusiasm in your actions and your ability to co-exist in blissful harmony with all around you. I am not saying it is all always well and good but you take what life throws at you. Unless you are awaken to this your music stays subdued and be mindful that you do not take this to your grave. Do not die with the music still in you. The world still wants to hear what you have to offer.

I have once been asked a question if I love and treat all my three children equally or have a favorite, and my response is that I loved them all the same, but I can only love them one at a time, similar to the analogy of picking up only one instrument at a time and enjoy the presence together. So it should be with every other person we encounter, be in the moment and give it your fullest attention, and you will feel the connective magic. Any relationship that is built on the foundation of trust and integrity is always a one-to-one encounter. Human feelings and emotions are delicate grounds to thread on and unless we invest the time and effort and be 100% in full presence, it will not be fruitful. There are no shortcuts in establishing strong and trusting relationships. It requires both character and competency, a skill with the heart of glorious wisdom.

Imagine if I pick up the Ibanez semi solid electric guitar and at the same time stand in front of the conga and bongo drums, and attempt to play both simultaneously. What music do you think would come out of it all. Probably some sounds will be made no doubt, but it will be at best 80% level of potential performance in each of the instruments. There will be only a mechanical action with no true spiritual connection. However, if I play each instrument individually my attention and connection is 100% and sometimes more. The first song may appear stiff but by the time you get to the third number you are already one with your instrument. As we come closer to the next station we move into the next spectrum of a higher spiritual dimension. Be open to taste this new offering. The term spirituality is not meant to have religious connotations although it can be if you are one who has chosen such a path. To the rest it simply means the truth. The truth does not need you to believe it, as it is always present regardless.

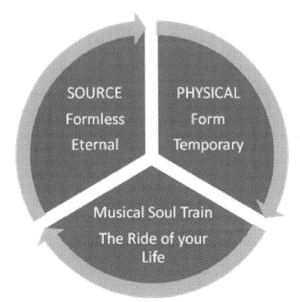

Station 5: A Spiritual Journey

Quote:

Our number one job here is not to be better than anyone else, but to be better than what we were before

STATION FIVE

A Spiritual Journey begins

By now you may have realized that the physical realm that we live in on planet earth has more to it, meaning there is a mirror that reflects the unseen realm. The formless nature like emotions and thoughts are real although we cannot see them, but we will feel the manifestation once it becomes actions or words spoken. Communication experts have taught us that effective interactions rely on the three components of words spoken, tone of voice and body language. Words spoken only account for 17% of the whole process. This says the unspoken portion tells a lot more. So the next time listen carefully to what is being said and equally important listen to what is not being said. In the silence of things, there lies much to be understood.

I see greater hope when I know things are beyond just the physical condition because what we associate through our senses only provide a small part of the equation. If the physical aspect is all there is, we will be literally "doomed" (as least in my view). If my whole life is linked to just my physical possessions and positions in life, I am vulnerable when these are taken away and it is a great possibility it can happen. If my self worth is dependent on the opinions of others I leave myself open to the whims and fancies of people I associate with.

When I meet an accident and curse the high heavens for the misfortune and then begin to experience more calamities, I will surely lose faith and hope. When I complain daily I will also attract more of the same predicaments which will lead me to continue complaining. Before you know it, it becomes a downward spiraling effect. Eventually I lose meaning and purpose, and when my time is up and my physical body returns to dust, my whole life would have meant nothing to me and those who were dear to me. This would be really sad. Eventually I will be disillusioned because I have not understood what lies in the overall scheme of things, the arrangements of the divine source and the power of the unseen realm.

Not surprisingly many behave this way and then they will blame the whole world for their current state of affairs. Thus over time their lives spiral downwards and will lose all hope and meaning. Unknowingly they are distancing themselves further from salvation and the way towards true meaning and happiness. In the teachings of Ho'oponopono (a Hawaiian wisdom teaching), the human mind only comprehends 2% of what is really going on around us. The other 98% works in a mysterious way and I refer to this as the response of the universe and laws of attraction. We will refer more to these teachings further on.

At the 5th station we are almost half way on life's journey. This is the phase when we shift from the morning of life to the afternoon of life. When we approach the late 40s and early 50s, our perspective of what is truly important changes, and this is an appropriate time to move into this mood of spirituality as a renewed foundation towards the WAY. In a research made on this age group, spirituality and service to others came out in the top five most important things surveyed.

This paradigm shift comes from asking the fundamental question of "who am I" and "what is my purpose here". I was born and raised in a home that did not insist on one particular religion that we were forced into. In my younger days I remember following my mum and grandmother to Buddhist temples, filled with joss stick smoke, and at the same time went to church on Sundays and on Christmas day and eventually I was baptized and got married in a Methodist church. My dad was a Methodist practitioner, my mum however was a Buddhist and we got along fine. My dear mother would pay respects in a similar way even at Hindu temples and goes to Church. To her, GOD was everywhere and she need not have to subscribe to just one manner of worship. Today I also follow the teachings of Mahikari, which means True Light, for the past 22 years and have been taught many new ways of how to manage our lives and understand the plan of God. I have since learnt to be open and take in all I can, as all righteous paths will lead to the truth. It is only when there are human interpretations that will make a mockery of the sacred teachings. So you need to discern for yourself what eventually is true for you in your adopted belief system and use it to develop your faith even deeper.

So my domestication at home allowed me to realize that we all have individual beliefs and we have no right to insist our beliefs upon another person, even on my wife or my children. What we respectfully should do is to allow them to explore for themselves, that there has to be a better explanation to the bigger picture of life. To do this, each person has to seek their own path and achieve self actualization. When we are born, we have a pre-ordained destiny, which may change depending on the choices we make at the cross roads of life. Life will throw at us many moments of joy and of course challenges, but how we navigate these turbulent waters has to be based on our values and the wisdom that we have learnt along the way.

Many actions that people take in their journey towards a spiritual path is engrained in firstly one's domestication, taught by well-meaning adults and what they encounter later on in life. Some are born into a particular belief system and they adopt it as part of the process of getting on in life. We do not know the fine tapestry that is ordained for us so I stay away from such discussions on any one particular worship methodology as I trust all religious inclinations are always for the better. In my own experience, there is a higher power, a higher intelligence and the following have been my pathways to knowing the WAY. I do not subscribe to just one practice but am open to all that is based on the universal principles of fairness and love. Be mindful that some interpretations are human interventions, and the truth may be distorted. I will leave it as that for the time being for your own conclusions. Dwelling in this topic would take another book and I choose not to indulge in these debates. To each his own I always say.

What does it mean to be Human?

My first encounter was a reading that I described briefly earlier on. We are a combination of physical and non physical. The form is what we call human, because we can see, feel the human structures and the entire anatomy in great detail with the advent of medical sciences. Then there is an invisible force that drives our heartbeat, our breathing and digestive systems, just to illustrate a point. When we go to sleep each night, do we consciously give instructions to our heart and lungs to keep on functioning and they are not allowed to take even a toilet break. Who or what drives this? It can only be an energy source that governs all things to be alive and flourish. The same source that gives us life, also feeds the birds, makes the flowers bloom and the sea currents flow. Such is the magnificence of the unseen force, yet totally present and pulsating each moment.

The unseen force or energy has to come from somewhere and is by essence formless, yet living and functioning. So the "being" in us has to be the formless part of the equation. Hence we are a combination of form and formlessness, the human side and the being. I must also repeat here that all things start from an energy field, as everything is energy. In our case the formless energy connects us to the highest realm of divine energy. The physical is a manifestation of 60 trillion cells that make us up on this planet, which we call the body, which is God's highest creation. In combination we are a human being.

In Dr. Dyer's book, **The Shift**, he taught us about the transition from NO WHERE to NOW HERE. Even before conception, there was an energy force waiting to manifest into that tiny protoplasm from the union of the sperm and the egg of the female form.

This gave me a perspective that I had not thought of before, as my education to this point in time was that the day life started was upon conception. Conception therefore was a physical form, only seen under a microscope. But a living energy was present even before that act towards conception. What an insightful thought, and truly fascinating.

Then the journey began and for the next nine months we did absolutely nothing (NO-THING), and yet everything was done for us.

Today on average we all have 60 trillion cells in our body and each cell knows exactly what to do. Ever wondered who trained them, who was their supervisor and were they ever given a bonus at the end of each year or even applied for vacation leave. No, they worked tirelessly and were governed by a higher force, a higher wisdom that allowed the natural progression of being and their creation. This is beyond any human comprehension to imagine what unseen power drives each of these 60 trillion cells.

So after the nine months of gestation, we all celebrated the birth of a baby, a new addition to the family. In a traditional manner we said "thank you" to whoever orchestrated all the events in the mother's womb, and we declared that we will now "take over". So the domestication process began and we all acted as if we had all the answers. How interestingly fascinating this is, have you ever wondered.

I came across this insightful passage that sums up what is it that we are here to experience on earth and perhaps offer a glimpse of our spiritual journey in this human body.

If human beings understood God from the beginning it would mean that they themselves were great deities. There would be no need for them to seek God. There is a certain order of things in the universe. To grow closer to him it is necessary to follow that order. God has arranged things so that any child of God who makes devoted efforts can grow closer to Him. This is part of the nature of human beings as Gods' children. A towering pine grows from a sprout which in turn springs forth from a small seed. An adult human begins life on earth as a baby. Making efforts is an arduous process and it can be difficult. It can even leave one out of breath. God has arranged things so that everything will grow. A sprout is light weight, but a full grown pine tree becomes heavy. The heavier the tree the more power is engendered in the roots and the stronger the tree's vitality becomes. This arrangement enables the tree to grow easily and become sturdy, and it can withstand rain and strong winds. The tree would never grow tall and strong if it did not need to bear a heavy weight. From ancient times it has been said that ease and comfort spring from ardor and hard work, and this gives rise to ease and comfort. People today think that happiness can be theirs without effort, but the truth is that happiness does not come without hard work. Only when people are ready to bear the weight should they attempt to lift it. Otherwise they will end up collapsing under it and be destroyed.

The above passage tells us there are ups and downs in this physical journey and is part of the natural process cycle, and we need to learn and accept this and make efforts in the quest towards true happiness along the way. The road to the truth will be truly tested ever so often and you will feel the challenges directly. How you manage the "testing" period will leave you stronger or otherwise day by day. Those who falter will have to pick themselves up. In times of adversity, take a look at your innermost attitude when you faced with a difficult situation or an event. It is important to understand more deeply the spiritual significance embedded within each phenomenon. We will deal with the topic in search of happiness below in more detail.

In Search of Happiness

What do humans really want? Is it a nicer and bigger house or a luxury car or more money in the bank, more travels on a first class ticket and a Caribbean sea-cruise? Ask some people and reflect on their answers. No judgment to be made. Just take it in. You will find that many are seeking to satisfy physical and materialistic needs. This is evident and those familiar with Maslow's theory of needs will understand this. My late father once told me, that there are only two kinds of people in the world, which are the "haves" and the "have-nots". So the "have-nots" will always want a bigger this and that. The "haves" surprisingly also want bigger this and that. This says we are never satisfied. We are indeed a greedy lot, and continue to chase materials. We are often spoilt for choices especially food that is in abundance and when it becomes a chore to decide what to eat and where to eat. Compare this to some countries where only one basic meal of rice a day is available and is cherished. Where is the rational to this comparison?

We have progressed greatly in the last 100 years, with quantum leap developments in the field of science, medical and social collaborations. Today the world is smaller with the likes of facebook, skype, whatapps, twitter and so forth. Communication has advanced so significantly which is truly amazing. We need not attend lectures to learn due to e-learning facilities. We can talk and see each other at the same time with video conferencing capabilities. With all the materialistic advancements, have we achieved true happiness? Search your soul for the answer. Have you? If not, why?

Allow me to offer an insight of what I personally experienced in the pathway towards happiness. If you really think about it, happiness is what all of us want to achieve here on earth. We want to create a heaven like "garden of eden" so to speak, where there are no wars and conflicts, and every person is fed and clothed comfortably and have shelters above our heads, and live in harmony with song and laughter. No more EGO trips that one individual is better or superior and respect for humanity and nature. This sounds like a dream. While we are here, wanting to change the world instantly which we cannot even conceive as possible in this lifetime, what we can do in our own power and circle of influence is to change ourselves. We are given the tools to do that. It starts with being healthy. Health is wealth because it allows you to use all your faculties to serve others, go about being in gainful employment, to be able to walk unaided so you do not burden your loved ones in the golden years. All of us seek health as an extension to prolong life. No wonder when we are "sick" we run to the doctors and hospital to "get well" so we continue to function in normal daily existence. True health is free from illness. The common cold and flu is still common (excuse the pun). It is a natural way to clean the body so let it be.

The second most important element in the happiness equation has to be harmony. We are not an island. Given all the wealth in the world and being isolated has no meaning to life. Wealth as we see it is often linked to unlimited excess to money. This is a short lived joy as the saying goes "money is only good if you do good with the money". Money is another form of energy, which if used appropriately will transform to another physical form which can help those in need.

We need to be united in love and harmony so that we are able to co-exist. In the human spirit we are from the same source and we need to have each other as companions, as spouses, parents and children, relatives and friends and work colleagues to thrive. It is through these interactions that we find fulfillment. Life is not to be lived in isolation, but in oneness. Being in harmony requires each one to respect the other as a child of God, as a divine soul with the same ambitions and has every right to be happy.

Life in harmony is likened to a 100 piece full orchestra with a myriad of musical instruments and when played under a skilled conductor produces beautiful angelic music that touches your heart. Each musician is an expert in their own instrumentation but yet they are able to combine in unison under the watchful eye of the conductor. When there is total harmony you hear one magical presentation because of the blend of differing instruments come together but played in the same key. The musical experience is out of this world. There is a synergy that produces 1000 violins in perfect harmony.

Similarly in life, we are our unique selves, with our own talents, yet we can create magic when we blend in with others, in spite of differing opinions and preferences, but able to place others first by being humble and serving humanity. Imagine if one member in the orchestra decides one day he would like to play his own style and pace, or in a different key because he prefers it. He alone then will disrupt the entire ensemble and the entire 100 man band would have been destroyed. That is exactly the same in human history and we have seen many who are the greatest orators and convincers, but have led many souls down the path of destruction. Aldolf Hilter was one such example, of a leader who inspired others and we see some even today in the modern world. Dictators who control their citizens with an iron hand to do their bidding will not be tolerated at the end.

The harmonious theme is sought after in all families, between husband and wife, parents and children, work places, team sports and even those running the government of the day, to create a positive atmosphere that brings out creativity, passion, beauty and love to its citizens. We are the citizens of human history.

The third ingredient in this pie called "happiness" has to be prosperity, and not in the context that you require millions of dollars before you say I am happy. The feeling of prosperity comes from feeling grateful for the material blessings we enjoy today, the food on the table, the money in the wallet and a roof over our heads and perhaps even some small savings in the bank. When you are in the realm of saying, I need more to be happy, you will be disappointed because it is a wrong feeling tone you send out. Negative feeling tones declare to the world that you feel "lack", you find scarcity, there is a "never enough" thinking which will never manifest into any improvements. "I will only be happier if I have a million dollars in my bank account". This mean your happiness is dictated by a future event that may not even happen for you. This is dangerous territory to venture, and many will get hurt and disillusioned. You spend a lot of energy to chase the things you want and after you get it, you feel you want more. A thought comes to mind and tells you, you have spent so much effort on this endeavor and you deserve more. It never stops, and then more becomes less. The correct feeling is one of gratitude and has an abundance mindset. Allow others to rush to the buffet spread. Your turn will come eventually, and there is still plenty left.

In essence, health, harmony and material well being are the ingredients to become truly happy. Any one element that you miss out will elude happiness in your life. Imagine you have millions but a broken home, with constant conflicts with family members. If you are a tyrant parent, your children may secretly wish you were dead so they can inherit the millions. Same goes when you are always sick, you cannot even use money to seek pleasures in travelling. There are many who have riches but of poor health, failing eyesight, and losing teeth. Can you still enjoy the foods you love?

We need to offer a debt of gratitude if we are able to get up daily, get dressed, walk out the door, go enjoy a hearty breakfast and earn a decent day's wages. Do yourself a service this weekend and visit a person in hospital and you will walk out a more grateful person enjoying life's simple blessings. Try it!

Events currently manifesting in the modern world

The second most eye-opening encounter will be the events that happen all around us. Open the newspaper or turn on CNN channel on TV and what do you see and hear everyday. I am sure you can list a ton of events, but focus on two extremities. One aspect will be all the news and advertisements that will portray very positive energies. Invest for your future in good education, staying healthy, own properties and cars, buying the latest and greatest electronic gadgets and many more. What attracts us is the hopefulness of a better life, a life that is laid on a golden path and is portrayed as heaven on earth. The other aspects of a good life are celebratory events, hosting of dinners and graduating ceremonies as examples of positive events which are filled with joy and laughter.

Then on the other extreme, you will see new conflicts arising, ongoing wars, presidential debates and politicians telling who is better than whom, with fault-finding being the theme, thefts, rape, earthquakes, accidents, hunger, work strikes and many more. These portray the other emotions, and we can put labels such as sadness, worry, disgust and even the high ego being manifested.

In between you also have some reflection opportunities. Articles and books are written on managing self better, improve your thinking that would help the world be a better place, care for the elderly and doing charitable work, serving others before self. These are the middle path views we see. But notice that these only account for a small percentage of the readings made available.

If you consolidate all the above events what comes out very glaringly at you? Do we see positives and negatives that cancel each other out? Do we question why such disasters are happening? Why is the human EGO so high? Why do we fight and kill each other? Is happiness an illusion? Nothing is permanent. I am sure you have some other insights as well. How can everyone live in peace? Is it a dream too far?

My reflection is that everything that happens is for a reason. There are no coincidences. Every act that happens is a choice that is given to the human race. Compared to nature, which is designed to perfection, humans take on a different pathway, which is also by design based on self greed and self benefitting actions. Humans were allowed choices by God. Every choice has a consequence. History has shown us that with the great wars of our times, the human suffering continued because of this need to conquer and oppress others. But strangely enough, the human with his vast intelligence sometimes never learn to live in harmony with each other.

Let us now explore nature a little more. The sun rises each day, bathes all who chooses to come out in the sunshine. If you choose to stay in darkness, it is no fault of the sun. The wind that blows allows pollination to take place, and at the same time dries our clothes. The bees and insects start their day, busy but serene. The jungle which seems chaotic on the surface is in reality perfectly balanced, with low shrubs and tall tress that keep the moisture in balance. In the sea, big fish eat smaller fish, and there is no drama in that. In the Sahara desert, living creatures survive as they are built for the harsh environment, no complaints. Everything in nature moves in accordance with the flow of intention, as it was built for.

In fact nature is our survival partner and the more we go against it we will see the consequences eventually. We see clear evidences today that when we have exploited nature, we have paid back with more natural disasters. When we misuse what is given to us, there is a negative karma that is built up and this negativity has to find its way out. Energy can never be destroyed so it will manifest to release its built up power in some form, including earthquakes, floods and unusual weather patterns.

I believe that if we take nature out of the equation, humans will perish very quickly, but if we remove the human equation, nature will survive forever. So we have to understand what we are doing to this planet. A lot has been said on climate changes, saving the environment and what have you. In reality there is a threshold that only so much can be stretched before it breaks. The events we see today tell us that the breaking point is already here, and we have only a little time left to make a U-turn. In the bible, we hear of the end of the world, the Armageddon, the last days as they say. It may be like a light bulb that is fused and all this becomes instant darkness, and the clouds of darkness are looming above, so we need to be mindful and wake up from our dream of serenity. The world is facing turbulent times, which was predicted by many sages more than 50 years before. But who listens? We take many things for granted.

What matters most?

In the various disciplines that I have encountered one came as an interesting metaphor of managing the BIG ROCKS of your life. If there are BIG ROCKS then there will also be pebbles, and I could best relate this to perhaps the 10,000 things that Lao Tzu refers to. Therefore we have to ensure that the pebbles do not overwhelm us as we leave no more room for the BIG ROCKS. So what then are these ROCKS? For me it is about having the truly important things in my life placed on priority, and these have to be linked to the 4 dimensions of life, that is, the physical, mental, emotional and spiritual segments. Today in my afternoon of life I have made the following my BIG ROCKS, in no particular order as they are all integrated towards a life fulfilled with meaning and purpose. The ROCKS will cover spirituality, peace of mind, family, spirit of service and connecting to GOD's thinking.

Today's world still centers on materialism. You see it all around and we are urged or enticed to have bigger and better homes, multiple properties and fatter bank accounts, latest gadgets and improved models of cars to TV sets. The latest and greatest are in the media 24/7. While the development of material science has progressed significantly, it is now a time for a U turn to place lesser emphasis on material accumulations. Take stock and be happy with what we have. The wars that are still prevalent are based on territorial rights, and who has the authority to own what. Developed nations fight over a small island in the middle of the ocean. What is going on? Larger nations want to tell smaller ones what to do, and the list goes on.

On our home front, do you have peace of mind? Do we look for more when we actually have enough? Are we still chasing the next good thing on the market? Do we feel deprived when we do not have the latest and greatest. You be the judge of that. If you are not at peace with your current actions then you had better ponder the next steps. The rock of any person is their support system, either from their spouse, children, or siblings. Harmony in family relationships is crucial and we must protect the sanctity of this connection. The family concept also extends beyond the home. We need to secure our other families in the workplace, our social establishments as well as in worship circles. Without these bonds we will not be able to weather the storms. We rely on each other to give us the strength to pursue our higher calling.

We can observe that society has taught us to fend for ourselves, as my parents told me that the world out there is a cruel one. "No one cares for you so you better look after yourself" they said. All parents, I would dare speculate, would have strived and provided a better opportunity for their children than what they themselves had. This is no crime and is definitely a noble thought. We need to be mindful that such actions do not go overboard and that money does not grow on trees. Even if you have a money tree in your home, teach the correct values, because this will be for their own good and steer them in a right path. Believe me they will thank you for it in their later years. Children born with a silver spoon need to be taken care of because they have been overly protected and have no survival edge compared to street smart kids.

Thinking as God thinks is another important facet of the spiritual journey. If nature is to be your teacher, it will show you one thing. It is in perfect harmony and there are no earthly masters to guide them. Each role is respectfully ordained and all creatures abide by it in an accepting way. Humans on the other hand, are here to question every single thing and make a judgment based on their perceived knowledge. We need to be more accepting especially matters on principle-centered practices and the laws of the universe. There is nothing wrong with wealth as long as we seek the balance and understand where materials play its role. The final piece of the puzzle is to ask the pertinent question, what else then is there to achieve after all my worldly accomplishments and success stories and all my 10 houses and 100 cars, which has a special garage made to store them. Remember such joys are temporary, as you cannot cradle your Ferrari to sleep in the absence of a loved one when you need it most. With all the riches we accumulate we need to be at peace as well and in harmony with all of creation. True happiness is when we have attained the combination of health, harmony and prosperity. Gratitude for all things becomes basic guidelines for a meaningful life.

The spirit of service is far lacking in all aspects of life. My bias is that it operates from an EGO state of being. When we see ourselves as more important, more superior to others, more highly educated and having a top paying job, why would we want to serve others? We should be served instead, not the other way around. When we think this way we violate the fundamental rule of nature. Being of service is not about bending backwards to the whims and fancies of others, although some of us do it, but it is not done out of love. Majority of actions is done based on fear. We often do things for higher levels of authority because of the need to stay in the good opinion of others, or done to avoid punishment. The true spirit of service has to come from love of doing as a sincere gift to others. All else are superficial and has little spiritual energy. Small gestures go a long way. Holding the lift for someone rushing, allowing a car to cross ahead of you, a greeting, a smile are all service oriented actions. Service requires a tinge of humility and sometimes taking the lower seat. It is accepting new tea, and you need to lower one's cup below the teapot to receive the new tea. It is as simple as that. Simple in thought but seldom practised.

The ingredients for happiness (mentioned above) integrated together with identification of the BIG ROCKS provides a firm foundation for us to face the world head on. I am suggesting these spiritual practices to prepare one to navigate the fog that may blind your pathway. Be watchful as we now head on slowly into the next station.

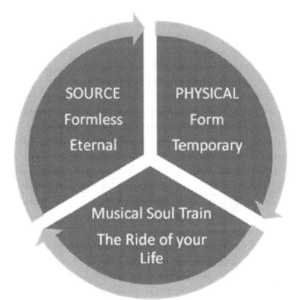

SOURCE
Formless
Eternal

PHYSICAL
Form
Temporary

Musical Soul Train
The Ride of your
Life

Station 6: The Fog

Quote:

What you are seeing and hearing right now is nothing but a dream. You are dreaming with your brain awake.

STATION SIX

The Fog

The world is an illusion. Everything you see is not real. Do not believe what others tell you. Do not even believe yourself. These are indeed strong statements which need reflection and further deliberation. Let us explore what is behind these meanings. When we encounter a fog, our vision is limited and we can only see probably just a few feet in front of us. Beyond that it is unknown because we cannot have a clear line of sight. When we are caught in a fog, we thread cautiously because we are fearful what is in front of us.

In this station the cold morning mist develops into a deep thick fog. The fog is a metaphor that blinds us from the truth. Reality is blocked off and it is left to the imagination what lies ahead on the road. Unless you have travelled this road before, the fog will disorientate you. For what you cannot see there will always be doubt, and you either retreat or push forward with courage and blind faith, or move steadily with a "knowing" that you will be watched over and cradled in the arms of the divine.

All of us, well almost, only believe what we can see, touch and smell. The common thing we often hear is that "seeing is believing". What we cannot see is considered "suspicious". I have heard a surgeon saying that he has done hundreds of surgeries in his career, and he has never found a soul. By the same token we can also ask a brain surgeon if he has ever seen a "thought"? We will subscribe that in general we do think a lot, because this is the mental faculty that we have been endowed with. As a man thinks so shall he be. While thinking is needed, we often "overthink" and make judgments on matters beyond our comprehension. The power of thoughts are fundamental in the initiation process, however we must appreciate how we think. Most of our thinking are based on our domestication which we will discuss more later on.

Another good example is that everything is made from basic building blocks of an atom, that combines together to form molecules and eventually cells. If you look at an atom, it is a circulating energy of electrons around a nucleus. From this perspective, it is a vibratory element. I will now tell you that everything vibrates, but only at different speeds. A block of wood appears solid because the vibration is much slower, so it seems solid. Even your skin appears solid, but under a microscope you can see a different picture altogether. In terms of vibratory speed, the following is a range from slow to fast: it starts with solids, followed by sound energy and then light energy, then a thought and ultimately spirit.

Ever wondered why you see a lightning bolt and a few seconds later only hear the boom sound. It tells you that one travels faster than the other. At the top of the range are thoughts and then spirit, although I have not seen the speed of a thought being measured. So the first fog to overcome is to surpass only believing what we can see, hear, smell and touch.

In the writings of Don Miguel, the author of **The 4 Agreements**, he talked about the smoky mirror. The reference is made to the material frame we relate to and navigate in daily living. We relate to the frame as who we are, by our given name, our role we take on, the titles we hold and the accomplishments achieved so far, not forgetting the type of car we drive, the house we live in and the club memberships we join. All these references are the trapping that make our reality and stops us from recognizing who we really are. Hence he (Don Miguel) refers to this illusion as a smoky mirror. The Toltecs (a Mexican tribe) believe we are all **light**, and we are formed from light source. When there is smoke we fail to recognize the light and fail to recognize others in their true essence.

With that smoke we cannot even see who we really are. Putting this into perspective, human beings are stuck in a maze, the maze of human suffering. Let us list some examples for thought:

The Smoke: We are taught from young to be fearful of punishments and crave for rewards. Thus we act based on such motivation. We act not from the heart but driven by expectations of opinions of others.

The Truth: Be aware of the domestication that limits your actions. Never act from a fear base approach, because these are weak energies. Strong energy is to believe in your actions that are inspired by truth, and do your best each time.

The Smoke: In order for other people to listen to me I need to show them who is the boss. I will show my authority and displeasure directly to the staff, and they will respond in future.

The Truth: Respect cannot be demanded, it has to start with a change that you are willing to make. Treat others with respect but at same time, be honest with your feelings. You do not get what you want, you get what you are.

The Smoke: I am successful based on the millions I have made holding a high level position in the company and the material possessions I have invested in.

The Truth: Your self worth is not based on your possessions and other material tokens. What you have today you take nothing with you. We all return to source the same way we came, and that is with absolutely nothing. Your self worth comes from the heart of giving and service to others. When you do this you find meaning and purpose in your life.

The Smoke: My achievements are due to my personal efforts and today I am a much better person than most people. I have studied hard and deserve all my successes.

The Truth: You have been given a healthy body so that you can use it for work, and offer gratitude each day for the blessing. True happiness comes from being healthy and in harmony with all living beings. I am a better person than what I used to be. My responsibility is not to change others, but to change myself.

The illusion tells us we are humans born to suffer. The FOG prevents us from recognizing our true self, which is divine and with immense potential, because of where we came from. Again to remind ourselves, we are made of 60 trillion cells and each one is capable of doing exactly what it was destined to do. What drives these actions, if not for a higher power? When was the last time upon falling asleep you consciously told your heart to go on beating or your lungs to function as you laid down to rest. Almost never, I would presume and yet everything was done for you. Therefore be mindful when you tell yourself you have limited capacity, because it is self talk that is building a fence around your greatest potential. By removing this limitation in your thoughts, your "wishes" can be fulfilled to do whatever your heart desires.

For things to CHANGE I have to CHANGE first.

I would now offer some possibilities for you to consider on your journey towards higher levels of awareness. The irony is that as we get older we become more stubborn in embracing change. As we get older we presumably get wiser, that is what we always think. Some only get older, period. Wisdom comes from being open to all possibilities. We are often the last person to change, as we expect others to change first. This is purely wishful thinking. The only person you can initiate change is yourself. Consider the various views offered below when you navigate the possible changes in your life. Each view offers a different approach and appears separated at first and yet will be eventually connected.

View 1—our higher self

We were created from the highest wisdom, the same source that created the solar system and the galaxies. This expansive creation is in us, and we only need to tap into it. Allow the pure potentiality to surface. The same intelligence that looked after us in the womb for 9 long months does not do this miracle act and then abandons us. As a creation of the highest realm, there is residing inside all of us a greater person who is waiting to reveal itself. What are you waiting for? Tap into this internal force to accomplish more. You just have to want to and start the process of change. It is only a thought away.

View 2—light and love

We are light, pure light and pure love. Where did this concept of light surface. I must say this reference came from my association with divine light energy. Light is associated with darkness, and only when we encounter darkness we appreciate the light. Without darkness the concept of light has no reference point. The dark days are ones that we feel down, sad or having a feeling of unpleasantness. When you enter a dark room you have no direction. Your first instinct is to find the light switch. When we feel down emotionally or otherwise, where is the "light-switch" in you?

View 3—mental awareness

We claim to know everything around us by using our mental capacity. Yes even though the brain is a magnificent creation in reality we know less than 2% of events and phenomenon that affect us. We are not aware or even realize that the other 98% has been planned for us, and beyond our mental boundary. The 98% works in the invisible side of the physical world. Everything that manifests in the physical realm has already been patterned spiritually. Suspiciously scary but true. Therefore stop thinking too much. Let go and let God in. Trust in the now of things and go with the flow.

View 4—power of thought

Everything that manifested in its physical form started from a thought. Your mobile phone today started with someone years back with an idea, a thought. Thoughts are vibrational energy that is faster than the speed of light. Combined thoughts will generate a mass of energy field that can affect change. Gregg Braden, in his writings, suggests to us that a shift in energy can start by having the square root of one percent on a given population to start the process. So for a community or population of 10,000 people, it only takes 10 persons to do this. If 10 persons focus on a single thought the energy field is activated. For the less mathematical savvy folks, 1% of 10,000 equal to 100, and the square root of 100 is 10. This is also seen in the power of group prayer.

View 5—energy flows

The practice of Tai Chi or Qi Gong, are ancient arts that teaches us how to tap the energy around us. This practice subscribes to us as having meridian channels that run through our body. Acupuncture practice also uses these same points for activation of chi or energy. Having good chi flow enhances the human body's capability for self healing. Our body was already created with a self healing system, but modern life styles combined with higher pollutants in the air we breathe, the water and food we consume have dampened our channels of lively "chi". Qi Gong teaches us of the five flows in the body, which is blood flow, vibration flow, heat flow, neuro-chemical flow and electromagnetic flow, and these are in constant movement in our bodies.

To my knowledge no medical surgeon has ever seen a meridian point in his entire practice. These are the unseen spectrum beyond our normal human awareness.

The five views address the different dimensions and approaches to appreciate the formless nature and the power of the unseen realm. We first begin to acknowledge the greatness that lies within us when we subscribe to our connection to divinity, which has the nature of light and love at its core. If we come from the source of creation we have the potential to be what we choose to manifest. Our intention to manifest our wishes starts from our initial thoughts and is brought to action by projecting strong abundant vibrations that eventually move the energy patterns around us which is beyond our mental capacity and human comprehension. With these embedded divine entities the act of CHANGE has to begin with us, because we clearly see that subsequent changes will permeate the environment and other fellow humans, with us as the catalyst. Indeed for things to change I have to change first.

Keeping on course and mending the faith

The fog is the metaphor of an illusion that keeps you off track. The path you take is a long and winding road that may appear to lead to nowhere because of the fog. Imagine it as climbing a steep wall, which you scale up and it is easy in the beginning when your stamina is high and as you reach the half way mark, there could be slip-ups as you begin to tire. Similarly in your journey to reach a higher level of awareness, you may need to stop and rest, regroup your thinking and focus on the next move, and sometimes you move up two steps and fall back a step. You may even need to side step and not even elevate for some time. Nevertheless there is progress but it wears you down. If you are weak you will stop and even slide back. But you have to persevere. Just like a dedicated marathon runner, you continue to train and train and are ever ready for the next run.

This is also what GOD does, to test us every now and then for a spiritual marathon. This is not out of malice but of great love. Only the toughest will make it, and in these turbulent times we need to push harder in terms of spiritual understanding and elevation. Hard times are already at our doorstep and can get even tougher. Observe the daily news of world affairs and the natural disasters occurring around us. When you reach a new level do not be complacent and think it is now safe. Each achievement brings a new level of endurance which needs to be faced once more. This has to be understood clearly. These are the waves and nodes in our navigation journey called life. The important point is that we keep the spirit in true alignment of our purpose. Our strategies may change but the purpose is on track to return to our true nature of divinity. The progress you make is not per your timetable in the human clock, but determined by a higher source, just as you cannot demand a flower to bloom because you ask it to. It will do so when the time is right.

In the same token we must keep on with the faith that what we do is on the correct path. The end is not for us to determine because the road back to divinity is a long and winding one that eventually leads to the heavenly doors. Do not be naïve that we will be able to repent fully in this physical lifetime alone. There are no specific goals for spiritual gratification but as long as you are vigilant in your endeavors there is no last train out of town. The train you take is there when you are ready to board but do make haste. As you make sincere efforts, divine power comes forth to make it happen for you. You must be on track and be on board to ride that soul train onwards to another peak.

Transcending from material thinking to non form energy

Scientists have always been fascinated by research into microscopic particles and today it is declared that there is nothingness in the final analysis, after breaking down atoms to quarks and to the smallest form possible. What we have been taught in perceiving all our lives through the 5 senses as absolute reality has today been proven that there is much more in the unseen and the invisible. In the final analysis there exists an energy pattern which cannot be seen by humans with all our advancements of technology. The space that is between the electrons and protons orbiting the nucleus has wisdom. So what you can see is far from what is there. Again pure potentiality of a greater force is available to us if we know how to tap into it.

We have looked at several concepts that are toolkits for us to navigate the fog in our lives. Now that we have exposed our understanding to other possibilities and not be closed to them, we can then be ready to transcend into the next level of reality. In order to do this you need to start letting go. Letting go and thinking less is a good start. This will starve the EGO by just allowing and not forcing anything.

At the present moment you can use the conscious mind (that 2% of your awareness), in your mental capacity to make a choice to begin the CHANGE in you. You can decide to stay at your ordinary level of awareness or begin to tap on pure potentiality and change the way you look at things. In the way of ZEN, everything has life, and I view this as everything is energy. When you can appreciate the presence of energy you move with it, you embrace it with a knowing that it can only do good deeds if you tune in to the right frequencies. You become one if you match with the intentions of the universe. So as you pick up your guitar and play, you similarly connect to the spirit of the instrument, and magical music will be made. Simply said all of us carry a song inside us waiting to be played. It is this song that makes us alive as true humans. So start today to explore this gift in you. When we finally surrender our human EGO ways we will be able to seek the light within, so enjoy the next station coming in at the next corner.

SOURCE
Formless
Eternal

PHYSICAL
Form
Temporary

Musical Soul Train
The Ride of your
Life

Station 7: Seeing the Light

Quote:

Be like the sun who after all this while never says to the earth you owe me, imagine a love like that, it truly lights up the whole sky

STATION SEVEN

Seeing the Light

So is there a light at the end of the tunnel. There sure is. The light has been there since the beginning of time. We however choose to move into darkness, and have eluded the light for some time. Now is the right time to come out of darkness, and bathe in the light. Darkness is cold and damp and has low level energies. Imagine the dawning of each morning. The sunlight brightens up the whole sky. It gives light and warmth, and a new beginning each day. We stay in darkness when we are separated from our source, the creation of all. We must learn how to reconnect with source, which is our true essence.

This is the same inner light within you which is your guide towards the WAY. As Lao Tzu wrote this verse it allows us to understand clearly what is the path of Living by Your Inner Light. The verse written 2,500 years ago is reproduced below:

A knower of the truth
Travels without leaving a trace
Speaks without causing harm
Giving without keeping an account
The door he shuts, though having no lock,
Cannot be opened

The knot he ties, though using no cord,
Cannot be undone

Be wise and help all beings impartially
Abandoning none
Waste no opportunities
This is called following the light

Life is a wave of ups and downs, just as there is day and night. There is turbulence everywhere, but at the same time, there is also love and beauty in everything. How you choose to see them is the key in this journey we call life. What is your paradigm? How do you see what is happening before you? How you react will determine your final destiny. When you face a challenge, how do you react? What is your mind's eye on any situation you face? If you understand the truth as the verse suggests then you travel this path accepting all as it is. You begin to trust yourself and develop an inner code of conduct that is unwavering and aligned to universal principles such as gratitude for what we have, be of service to others, respecting all, judging none and honesty in delivering a good day's work. When you trust yourself, it is like travelling towards a destination with minimal planning and be in awe of what enfolds before you along the way. Thus the knower of the truth leaves practically no trial, as he leaves no marks. Living life is not to be done in each detailed step and planning but to take in each moment that you encounter as is. Live more spontaneously, pick up that guitar and start singing without inhibitions what others may think. When you live by the light you also waste no opportunities to be the instrument of peace and harmony. It is our choice how we live, either as a hostage to our EGO or to be a host to GOD thinking presence.

Let's start with a viewpoint when operating from an EGO state of consciousness.

- When things are well, this is my birthright to be.
- When I accomplish success, this is due to my hard work and my personal efforts alone

- When things turn for worst, you blame everyone else, it is always the fault of others
- When we fall sick, we blame God for not looking after us. We are a constant complainer.
- In a relationship, we take the upper seat, of EGO, barking out orders, being superior
- In order to be right, someone else has to be wrong
- We have to win every argument
- Demanding peace from others
- Demanding others to change their ways
- Since I am older than you, I have all the answers

The above viewpoints come from a paradigm of selfishness, whereby we fail to take any responsibility and will always push the blame to others, thinking we are always superior and can do no wrong. This also comes from a scarcity mindset that says there is never enough to go around so we have to have first rights and no consideration for others. On the other hand, a person who is operating out of God consciousness will look at it very differently, based on contrasting viewpoints as follows:

- When things are well, offer gratitude for the blessing
- When I am successful, I thank those who have been my teachers, for without them I will not be here
- When things turn for the worst, offer apology for any wrongful acts made knowingly or unknowingly
- When we fall sick, we are grateful it is not getting worst, our body tells us we need to rest
- In a relationship, we honor and respect others and we take the lower seat of HUMILITY
- When we are right, we choose to be kind and not "rub salt to the wound"
- When we have a choice in any conflict, we choose peace beyond anything else
- Be an instrument of peace in every opportunity

- When others do not change, be the change you desire to see
- After all this while I am beginning to see things anew and it is never too late to learn

Those who behave from an EGO state will have a lower destiny at the end of life because all the thoughts and actions are contrary to divine laws and principles. As one thinks so shall it be. A constant complainer will also have the opportunities befall him to continue in his complaining mode, and it feeds him constantly, and it fuels him to complain even further, to a point he will ask if there really is a loving GOD. It is impossible to contemplate GOD when you are not feeling GoOD about yourself.

Operating from GOD consciousness, we find joyful gratitude in everything and we will have greater blessings and reach a higher plane. In contrast there is a bigger GAP in an EGO operating state, because we move away from source spirit. We need to attain SATORI, the closing of the gap between humans and the divine. SATORI is the awakening that we need to have. Are all our actions taking us closer or away from source spirit?

Consider a plane flight with a destination that is 10,000 km away. If you start with a 0.1 degree error in navigation, you will have missed your final mark by perhaps 100 km or more, and land at the wrong place. Unless you correct the small deviation that is caused by wind or other elements, and be in a constant awareness mode, you will fall short heading towards the destination of happiness. So for those who live from an EGO based mode will fail to make the small corrections (a "testing" by God) and find that it is too late after 70 to 80 years, at your death bed, to say "have I got my whole life wrong?", then instantly die. That would be the saddest story ever!

Some spiritual practices tell us to be grateful that we are allowed to live each day. It is the power that allows our hearts to go on beating, our lungs to go on breathing and is never our own effort. The true essence of a human being is the synergistic combination of human effort and God's power. You can call it God, divine presences or source as being of the same reference. This originating source is all powerful and created the entire universe and the galaxies. It also created us.

Light is Love

Love cannot be truly explained or understood, it has to be felt. If you start to explain it, it is not love anymore, but an intellectual definition at best. When you invite LOVE into your hearts, wealth and success follows. LOVE what you do, and do it for the sake of others. We are born to SERVE. Live a life of service. We are born to share with no expectation, just like the sun, every minute of every day. It shines on everyone, no judgment, no choosing.

As the sun shines daily on my face, it warms my heart and bathes my soul, and does this every day, never asking for reward or expectations. With a love like this, it would light up the whole sky.

When we truly LOVE, we accept people as they are, and not what we want them to change into. Unconditional love says we will always love them irrespective what happens. There are NO conditions whatsoever. Motherly love for a child has no boundaries and no expectations in return.

Until we know how to LOVE ourselves, we cannot begin to love others, and as reciprocation, others cannot love us in return. When we cannot love ourselves, the negative vibration is also manifested that others are incapable of loving us as well. Everything therefore starts with us. Stop looking at others and outside for LOVE. In reality you do not need a partner to love you. You only decide to CHOOSE a partner because you WANT to and not because you HAVE to. Understand this fundamental point carefully.

Let us now explore some other facets of daily living which many of us face on a frequent basis. The topics are commonplace and we seldom pay attention over and above the surface views. I have selected random examples to illustrate the point and to offer a new view.

Handling FEAR

Modern teachings tell us there are only two basic emotions, which is Fear and Love. 90% of what we do stem from fear based thoughts and emotions. You may argue initially that this is not the case, but look carefully why you do what you do. Ask yourself can I choose not to do it? If it is a yes, and you feel absolutely no fear, then you are acting from a realm of faith and confidence, which is an act out of love.

Emotions that are frequently felt:

Fear of being cast out socially in relationships
Fear of losing your job
Fear of no income
Fear of losing a loved one
Fear of embarrassment
Fear of negative opinions
Fear of looking foolish in front of others
Fear of not having a place to live
Fear of people rejecting us, others saying NO to our ideas
Fear of rejection by management, by your family
Fear of people saying we are not good enough
Fear of fear itself
Fear of dying

Events that happen are neither good nor bad, as we cannot see the total picture, but only a fraction of it.

Therefore, any event that happens, just accept it and be in the moment to accept and move on. Allow the flow to be, no anticipations, no expectations. Just **let it be**. The Beatles got it right with their hit song.

The MIND became our greatest obstacles because we use it in a conscious state to make decisions. Most of the data comes from the sub-conscious so we need to STOP ALL THE PROGRAMS coming from past memories, which are old data. We NEED to clean this via

Ho'oponopono, a mystical Hawaiian technique. "I am sorry, Please forgive me, I thank you and I love you" are the four simple affirmations. If you are interested, pick up a book titled **ZERO LIMITS** by Joe Vitale. We neither understand nor control 98% of what is happening around us, but we use our intellect as if we know it all. This is the fallacy and the source of all anxieties, stress and problems we cause for ourselves. We need to stop this incisive thinking and what IF situations and what could go wrong. Allow inspiration to take over, and give the divine permission to manifest what is destined to be.

We rely too much of the 2% knowledge we have and take over the situation, which is the greatest misconception of the modern man. In fact we know very little, so we need to face reality. Human wisdom is derived from allowing a greater force to guide you. Human power is limited. When we realize this, we let go, and let GOD into our lives. The 2% should be used to be in the moment and then choose your next step FORWARD. There is nothing that can change the past, and there are no guarantees what will happen tomorrow. Use that 2% to be in the power of NOW, on this very moment, to make the decision and that is how it should be.

The conscious mind is aware of what we do and say, but the programs are coming from stored paradigms. These old files can be cleaned and we can make a choice to be better than who we have been. With the divinity within us we must contemplate what we want to be and feel that in your mind's eye. This will send a powerful force forward and sets everything in motion. Thoughts and actions need to be set up and manifested in order that creating the reality is possible. What happens then is beyond normal human comprehension. It is the 98% in constant motion that is of the greatest impact on circumstances surrounding you, and this is orchestrated by divine arrangements and intelligence.

FEAR becomes our main reason for our actions but we seldom see that it comes from over analyzing everything, and we have too much internal dialog with ourselves. We worry about the future that may never happen. Even if it does, what can we do but deal with it when it comes to face us head on. We are most fearful when we feel insecure and doubt our own capabilities. We need to understand that what is happening to us is designed for us out of love and we actually have everything we need today. We need not seek more.

FEAR is what is in our minds, nothing more. So THINK less. One who has faith will have doors open for him that would come at the right time. Our intellect is our greatest enemy. We think we know more when in fact we know absolutely nothing. The intellect can only choose to let go or control, to be in the present moment or not, to make a conscious effort of the next step. The emotions come from the sub conscious, which are hard wired from young, our path of domestication. The subconscious carries all the past memories and learnt behaviors that make us a victim of the past. Let go of this history by cleaning them.

Practise being quiet and silencing your mind, and then re-energize your surroundings with positive vibrations of love and harmony. It is worthwhile repeating here that we must live a life of calmness and stillness. In any turmoil, we can choose to play up the constant disorientation which the EGO says is due to external elements and blame everyone else, or instead choose stillness, as it is the way of the TAO. In times of conflict, choose not to think about what is taking place and take a few deep breaths and come back to your calm center. The same goes for the good times as well. The ups and downs are just the same as they are external to you, as they are temporary. Never allow these emotions to sway you from the calm center. Remember that the "still" is the master of unrest. Always tell yourself "this too will pass". Any event will pass eventually. Let go. Let live. Let God in.

WHAT is a Problem?

"A problem becomes one when you believe it to be so, however the real problem is not the problem at all, but your reaction towards the problem becomes the real problem" . . . .

There are NO problems, you only think it.

We are masters of suffering and we react to everything, seldom stopping to reflect and not react. Our EGO says we must have the last say. EGO tells us that we need to place our self ahead of others, the "me" first syndrome. In a buffet spread I need to go first to get the best there is, which works from a scarcity mindset. EGO is Edging God Out. It is superficial, and has no place in blissful settings. When we take things personally and do not clarify but assume the perceived reality, it likely causes pain and suffering and manifests itself as a problem. It is all up in our minds.

Learning to take 100% responsibility for everything that goes around you is a new paradigm, and act accordingly to clear the garbage that resides in the memories. We have two choices to make. We can blame others or take full responsibility for what you are attracting into your life. Either we live to our true being which is guided by a divine wisdom that brings us to act out of inspiration. Or, we live by our old programs and data that reminds us of the fear, sorrows, bad vibes that lock us down, and can never see a brighter day. People unknowingly start a day inviting more suffering because that is how they view themselves as victims. They also become judge and jury and gossip the entire day through. The next time you catch yourself gossiping, be aware of what you are doing.

Learn to be happy, it is our birth right. Discover WHO we really are. We come from a source that only knows goodness, love, compassion, beauty, joy, kindness and abundance.

Let GO and let GOD in.

Learn to FEEL GOOD, (feel God).

We were each created PERFECT. Perfection means no memories, no beliefs, no attachments and no judgments. Remember that nothing is what you think it to be. It is an illusion. Memories come from ancestors and past events. Clean these out and allow inspiration to guide us. We lose connections because our LINK is contaminated, and we need to clean this cord that connects us to the higher wisdom.

So we have to clean 24 hours a day, as suggested by **Ho'oponopono** practices taught by Dr Hew Len. Because our memories are playing all the time, it affects our thinking and emotions even we are unconscious about it. The act of "cleaning" is to petition to the DIVINE, letting the EGO go and saying I am sorry, please forgive me. Return to zero state, where it all began. To forgive is divine. It is an act of pure love in all circumstances.

Quote:

Forgiveness is the FRAGRANCE that the violet sheds on the heels that have crushed it.

Forgive and free yourself from more hurt, and killing of the EGO that thrives on being right all the time, and thrives on judging others or just taking revenge (hatred). When you get hurt you immediately want justice. An eye for an eye is often considered. Learning to forgive is hard initially, as the anger within is very strong. With humility and reflection over time, forgiveness is easier to practise and it must be heartfelt. No window-dressing.

The intellectual mind does not know GOD, because it does not "see" anything. Only the subconscious mind can communicate with GOD, through the super conscious level and then to divinity. Humans are a proud bunch and being a superior species among other creatures and living things, makes us quite arrogant. This is an illusion to the truth as we are all designed with a universal intention and we need to play our God given role, not a role that humans have interpreted by their own design. This is the great EGO—"Edging God Out" that is manifesting when we think we are above God. Thus be mindful that we do not draw from past memory as it gives you misleading thoughts and wrong actions, which stems from the fear in us and we stop moving forward because of the baggage of past doings and memories.

What is Divinity, the source and beginning of all things?

Quote: The mind does not know it, the heart understands it, the soul has never left it, so welcome home.

We are born into this world and enter this physical realm and we start to explore and allow our 5 senses to guide us and feel what the world offers us as we are in our journey called life. This path needs to be travelled no doubt. We garner experiences, emotions, love, hate, joy and sadness and what have you and this becomes our reality. After a while we seek more understanding on higher levels of thinking and awareness and will come back to the place of origin and begin to know it for the first time. The past history however does not let go. It is stored in archives in our sub-conscious mind. It stays there and often resurfaces automatically and brings past emotions to bear. It is this history that pulls us back and we never move forward. We get sucked in the past memories and it weakens us because we refer to it so often it is like a 10-ton load preventing us from taking a forward step. Every time we come across an event or even a person whom we have had bad experiences with, we allow the inner judge to haunt us.

Therefore the sub conscious has to be taken care of, the inner child has to be loved and be taught to let go. The data is with the inner child. The inner child is the source of our emotions. Connect more with our inner child and love it. Teach to let go and let God in. We have this secret available but we never use it. We never knew what we never knew. This is unconscious incompetency, which is ignorance and bliss at the same time.

What is MONEY?

Money is a form of energy. Having money is not a bad thing but putting it in high priority is not good perspective. Money has to serve us and we must avoid being a slave towards money. Money is energy borrowed and has to be returned in some form or other.

When we stop having expectations we let go and have trust that GOD provides for us, and that we already have abundance each day. This form of realization stops our attachments towards money.

Whenever we do a task, do not attach it to any expectation of outcome or reward, but do it based on the fact that it feels right and it is benefiting others. It is an act of service to others before self. When we serve others as God's children we are doing what God wants and that itself is the greatest reward. Do it because of our love for Him, and not for the love of the money. When we do it otherwise (just for sake of money) it is always short term and brings little joy.

We will always get what is needed for our sufficient use and we need not use our intellect too much or worry too much, as we can only perceive less than 2% of what is been arranged in the spiritual realm. 98% of all other happenings we cannot perceive with the intellect. The 98% belongs to the world of divine arrangements, and it works in mysterious ways unknown to the common man.

What we experience are only fragments, it is never the whole story, so do not worry. Stop thinking too much. Stop our internal dialog. Give permission to allow divinity to guide you, allow the flow to be. Do not be too intellectual in analyzing everything and over stressing oneself. We are never in control in the first place so why be so stressed out. God's timing is always perfect and we should not expect otherwise.

Always clean, because we are 24 hours in turmoil without even realizing it, so we need to say sorry for whatever is in us that is causing this pain or event in our lives. We come from memories from ancestral lines so we have much cleaning to do. Ask for forgiveness for all past events and memories that caused us pain and suffering and then love our inner child, and accept it as an integral part of us. Once we clean, we connect to the super conscious and hook up to inspiration.

As we sleep give thanks for everything and love God as He loves us unconditionally. We have much to be thankful for. Thank you and I love you. Clean, clean, clean, and allow inspiration to come in and guide us with wisdom. Return to divinity at zero limits where we all came from. ZERO is the state of true purity. Be happy, it is our birthright. So claim it. It is the easiest way. Happiness is a state of BEING, the state that you are intimately connected to. With God's blessings, we can have a great human experience.

Everything that has been shared so far requires you to be at a higher level of awareness to appreciate this new view and truth to all. What does this mean? Imagine you are at the side of a mountain and all you can see is at the ground level. If you choose to stay here you cannot see beyond the trees, and the trees become your reality and your current state of awareness. The reality of your world is that there are only those trees that exist because that is what you can only see every day. And that is it. If I tell you there is more beyond, you cannot see them and therefore have difficulty in believing me. If you decide to move up to another station perhaps 100 feet higher, you now can see a little more. Moving up 100 feet is not difficult but staying at 100 feet is the real challenge. Unless you are firmly embedded you may slip occasionally and fall several feet down. This is where you become disillusioned when some event or disaster rocks you and believe me there will be many such events along the way. Until you secure yourself firmly only then you can consider the next 100 feet to the next station. This allows you to now have even a further view. I remember watching a replay of the Aceh tsunami of 2004 that was filmed by personal footage of survivors. You could see that people on higher ground were aware of the huge waves moving rapidly towards the shoreline but those at ground level were oblivious of the danger. Those on higher levels were shouting for them to run but to no avail, as those at shore level could not perceive the danger and were too far away to hear the warnings by others. This analogy gives us an idea of being at a higher awareness level when we need to be, so that we can navigate the "tsunamis" that life throws at us. I do not profess to have reached the highest level or even close, but I have attempted to climb each step as best as I can, and this takes time, patience, listening, observing, contemplating, reflecting and praying for guidance. I have been at it the last 10 years and still continuing to learn with all humility. This is what I am encouraging you, to move a little higher to contemplate a newer view that perhaps will change how you see things as different and change your perception. By navigating to a higher plane you will see beyond the FOG that keeps you from seeing the light and the truth.

Living on Purpose

The Kalahari bushman talks about the two hungers. First there is the little hunger which is to feed their belly with food provided by their environment by hunting and planting and also with basic clothing. They can exist daily with these basic needs. However there is a greater hunger, which is to live a life of meaning and purpose. The greater hunger if not fulfilled makes life meaningless. In the study of Maslow hierarchy of needs, he talks about a pyramid, where at the bottom spectrum of the structure all humans begin their basic wanting from the foundational need of air, water and food for day to day survival. Without air we will be dead in 3-5 minutes, without water 2-3 days. These are the minimum basic needs to stay alive. At the next level of human need, it is about having a roof over your head, a shelter and clothes to wear to keep us warm, and then further up the pyramid comes the need of feeling loved, being in a relationship, having a job to earn money and achieving a certain status in life. Many stay at this level of thinking and want even more possessions and wealth. A roof over your head starts with a small house and then aims for a large mansion. Then next comes all the luxury cars, airplanes and higher trappings of modern living, with more money, possessions and accumulation over time. There is nothing wrong with that goal if it makes you a happier person and is achieved sensibly. But at the top of the pyramid, there is a tiny space which is the point called purpose. This top point is normally not considered when we are attracted by all the luxuries around us. It is after enjoying everything there is, we still find a missing goal to what life is all about. The question then becomes, what is my purpose here? It is worthwhile repeating here that we come from no-where (formless energy) to now here (form and physical), and eventually return to no-where. When we return we take absolutely nothing (no-thing) with us, so what then is life's purpose, if we accumulate so much and take nothing eventually when the life ends on this planet? Even if you keep for your children they too take nothing when their time is up, and there is no guarantee that your hard earned wealth would stay as is. The answer then lies in giving. Be a giver. Many start by accumulating and when we are in the evening of life, there is a realization that we take not a cent when we go to the graves, and we start giving it away. The philanthropists do this as they find fulfillment in doing their part and in helping others. But you need not wait to be in your 80s to do this. You can start today by thinking with an abundance mindset and do it within your means. It is the thought that is the key that manifests the action of being a giver.

As we leave this chapter, consider the following shift in your thinking as you contemplate the power of TAO, the source, the nameless. We have been brought up just like many others and we have been living at ordinary level of awareness. You have to make the choice if you want to move towards a higher self and increased level of awareness. In order for you to do this, you need to suspend your belief temporarily and be open to possibilities. Be mindful that some aspects may conflict with your beliefs but I urge you to be open to give it a chance to touch your soul. There are two sides of our being, one being the EGO side and then we have the sacred part of self, which is also the true self. EGO attaches itself to the physical side, including material possessions, status, position and titles, wanting to look good in the eyes of others, to name a few. The true self is non attachment to any of EGO's hold but to be just like where it came from, bearing beauty, kindness, love and abundance in creative wonder. When you realize your true self, you have come home.

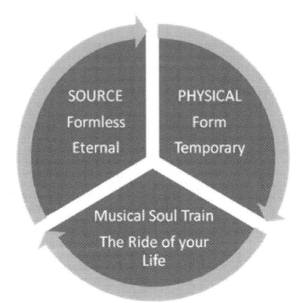

SOURCE
Formless
Eternal

PHYSICAL
Form
Temporary

Musical Soul Train
The Ride of your
Life

Station 8: Coming Home

Quote:

We often travel far seeking for the truth and we finally return to where we first started and begin to know the place for the very first time

Coming Home

After a while of exploration, we long to come home, because home is where the heart belongs to. It was your beginning and is your home base. Whatever adventures you may have been seeking, or some still looking for the answers, we need to come back to base camp. This is an important point, because HOME represents where those who love you do it unconditionally. They will love you for who you are, that same person born to this household. The people who love you do not see your riches (or lack of it), your accomplishments (or failures), your big titles and positions or the fact you own Park Avenue or only the shirt on your back. The HOME is both the physical space we have (our family) and also the inner true self that is connected to the higher dimensions. When the world outside gets a little too rough, when we are challenged we can always come back home, and be loved unconditionally. God loves us unconditionally.

Micheal Bubble's hit song HOME comes to mind. Taking one verse from the song it gives us a message.

Another summer day, Has come and gone away
In Paris and Rome, But I wanna go home
Mmmmmmmm
May be surrounded by, a million people I

Still feel all alone, I just wanna go home
Oh, I miss you, you know . . . .

The seasons come and go, we may travel far and wide, we meet many interesting people, but we feel we still have a connection to where we first came from, and we have a longing to return to . . . . our roots.

Our life journey starts physically the minute you left your mother's womb. The doctor helped to deliver and place you on your mother's bosom. Then the journey started and one day you leave home to seek fortune in the world. Many a young heart can relate to this. I was too a young heart, only today it is even younger. You tell yourself the treasure is at the end of the rainbow. As you chase the rainbow it disappears. It then becomes an illusion. The more you seek the more it will escape you. You meet many people along your journey and some may even become your close friends. In the end you may find loneliness and then you long for your base camp, where you can go back and recharge physically, mentally and spiritually.

Allow me to share a quote:

We seek the path of the world, spending countless years to look for the truth, not realizing we eventually find our way back to our beginning and know the place for the very first time.

The pathways we seek starts in the first 30 to 40 years where our ambition is for adventure and position and we see that as the pinnacle of our achievements. These are the goals in the morning of life. As we turn towards the afternoon of life, there is a shift to other priorities. As we enter our 50s, the number one priority for man has been spirituality, which never even made it to the top 10 preferences in the morning of life. We then ponder what we have been doing the first half century. Perhaps as we are nearing the return to source towards the evening of life, we have a renewed urge to look for the answer on "what is my life purpose?" When we start doing that we come to a place where we actually started, that was the point just before conception, from spirit to form.

This station is not the last one so we are far from calling it a day. Coming home simply means we have the opportunity to make a U-turn back to living a life with our highest potential yet to be fulfilled. This U-turn is not only applicable to those in the evening of life, but anyone who chooses to leave the EGO conscious state behind. EGO driven actions separate you from the source, and it becomes a FOG in preventing you to see the truth.

If you take a step back and ask, again the magic question of "Who am I?" I am source, or at least I am a part of source spirit and that this body that is given to me is a temporary container to house this eternal life force that does not die, because it was never born in the first place. What that was not born could never die. When you see this relationship, you begin to live again. So do not die with the music still in you. That is the tag line to fulfill your dreams and destiny because you have all the tools to do just that.

As a spiritual being in a human body, it will open up many doors, because you do not attach importance to the body which is just a shell. Your body does not define you. The opinions of others are their right to have, but it does not relate to you. It is just that they need to have an opinion, same as judgments made. They need to be a judge to have their own fulfillment. It is how they see their world. Some need to always be right, to have the last word in. You can free yourself from those bonds if you do not take it personally and you should not, because it is never about you. It is always about them to be who they perceive to be. In many cases they live and operate from a EGO conscious level.

So when you learn how to "die", that is to kill the EGO body focused paradigm, you then learn how to start living. This is shifting from EGO to GOD consciousness and shows you a whole new dimension that will leave you in awe. You will not need to be dependent on external factors to be truly fulfilled and happy. You eventually know who you really are, which is everything what the source is, and because you came from the same source, you have all the faces of intention. You are a drop from the ocean, and because you came from that source, you as a drop contain everything that the ocean has. Your potential comes from you as the "ocean in that drop". Just as a drop of blood, which has all the information on your being, if separated from the body will soon dry up and die. Because it is separated from source it will not flourish, and you are just like that drop of blood. If you are separated from your source you will also perish. When you reconnect to source you will begin to see the unlimited potential that the great wisdom has eternally existed from the beginning of time.

Here are some aspects you can consider as a paradigm shift in thinking and the words that you use:

From,

Winning every argument	to	everyone is entitled to an opinion
Using my position	to	doing by example
Telling others	to	listening more
I know best	to	what is your opinion
I make no mistakes	to	we are all human
I am always right	to	sorry it is my fault, I am responsible
Do it this way	to	would love to hear your inputs
We are superior	to	there is consensus in our way of doing
Come and learn	to	would you consider exploring alternatives
Eat this	to	would you like to try
Gossips	to	protecting the absent
Listen to me	to	can we consider this approach

The above example provides you a glimpse of the words we use and the self talk we do to ourselves. The spoken word has to be impeccable, because words can either "give life" or "destroy". So it is essential to "Think" before you speak. Words spoken need to be uplifting and even when you need to reprimand, scold with love. When we operate from a vantage point of love and respect, we will achieve the same outcome as intended as opposed of using hard tactics which leave a sour taste in the mind and hearts of others.

Words need to be impeccable—this means we should choose our words very carefully. Words have power, and how we use them have the ability to create, to uplift, or to destroy, to weaken or to demean someone. There is a Chinese proverb that my grandmother taught me, which translate to "if you have nothing meaningful to say, do not open your mouth and no one would accuse you of being dumb". When we encounter sages or wise men, they have little to say, as they have a knowing and avoid spending time in arguments and needless self talk. People who argue most are those who believe that they have to prove a point of being right, because there is a fear of being wrong. You will notice around you, words are loosely chosen and spoken. Some words are hurtful and may even come from those that are closest to you. When we take someone for granted we forget the art of communication. We slide into a time zone of normality, but the truth remains that each person is a soul and a child of God, and God does not speak loosely. In fact God speaks very little or not at all. Ponder upon this and hear your own spoken word in future.

In this U-turn back to your source, consider the following options to adopt:

The mastery of life is never a question of control, but of release. Only when you let go you can be free. We need to be free of attachments and physical accumulations. At this junction I would even say stop attaching to people around you, even loved ones. This is not to imply we stop loving them, no, far from it. It means that we have to see this life as temporary. While we are with them we give thanks and joy of fellowship. One of these days all of us will return "home" and although it will be seen as sad but it is not bad. There is an eternal way ahead. Just as my dad who would be 99 years if he were alive today had left me a legacy to mold my own path, and I similarly have let him go to do his own thing in the land of formless spiritual source. Letting someone go shows your love for them, because they too have their own journey. Imagine the pain of not letting go, it is tying you down forever. Let go and let them be. Life moves on for you too.

Find a balance between the human and the being. By now you would have heard that there is a spiritual side to everything. The human being is a combination of what appears as form (skin, bones, organs) and yet formless to the naked eye (molecules and atoms and quarks). We are a total combination of 60 trillion cells and a zillion atoms perhaps and in between the atoms is emptiness, a space where the electrons orbit the nucleus. So in summation we are NOTHING (no-thing). In form (physical, EGO state) you appear either superior or inferior to others. In non form you are neither. God consciousness is non form, but greatly influences the form. Hence your true self which is source spirit is the highest self of creation. This means you can do many things if you put your mind to it.

Be mindful of the energies surrounding you

We are surrounded by energies and they can uplift you or pull you down. Everything is energy. Even what appears as a solid is in fact energy, only difference is that these are slow energies so much so they appear solid to the naked eye. Unless you become aware you may not appreciate the influences of the various activities and other physical matter that are part of our daily lives. These unseen energies are very real and its power will affect you. Energies can be fast or slow, high or low. Sound energy is slower than light energy. Darkness are lower energies compared to light which are higher and faster energies.

Here are some areas to consider from an energy perspective.

Make prayer or meditation a regular practice in your life. You need to take time to get quiet, to go within, and from this silence make conscious contact with the source of intention. You're already connected to everything that you perceive as missing from your life; go with a realignment of purpose and intent. Sincere prayers and meditation are high energy patterns which are uplifting.

Become conscious of the foods you eat. Foods high in alkalinity such as fruits, vegetables, nuts, soy, non yeast breads and virgin olive oil are high-energy foods and will strengthen you, while highly acidic foods such as flour-based cereals, meats, dairy and sugars lower energy and will weaken you. The saying of you are what you eat is never more true.

Retreat from low-energy substances. Alcohol, cigarettes, caffeine, sugar and virtually all artificial drugs, legal or otherwise, lower your body's energy level and weaken you. Avoid excessive medication whenever possible. We pop pills for every little ailment, for a headache, a flu or a cold. Medication is never eradicated completely from your body.

Become aware of the energy level of the music you listen to. Some rap music—filled with profanity and messages about killing, for example—is an energy drain, while music that has a more soothing impact on the soul has been proven to be beneficial.

Become aware of the energy levels of your home environment. Make your home a nurturing, cheerful and peaceful environment. Be the one who provides brightness by warm greetings every day.

Reduce your exposure to low-energy commercial television. Children see 12,000 simulated murders on TV before their 14th birthday! Television news puts a heavy emphasis on the bad and the ugly, leaving out the good. Be selective in your viewing, and be a gateway to disallowing negative flow.

Enhance your energy field with photographs. Every photograph contains energy. Carry and display photos taken in moments of happiness, love and receptivity. Display uplifting quotations and other wisdom teachings that you can see visibly.

Become conscious of the energy levels of your acquaintances, friends and extended family. Choose to be in close proximity with those who are empowering, who see the greatness in you, who feel connected to spirit.

The above practices are not exhaustive but will provide you a framework of surrounding oneself with the right energy patterns. In addition be in constant gratitude mode for each moment and ask that you are allowed to serve others, and be in a position to do so in good health and be in constant harmony to all living things and nature. When we are able to reach this juncture in our journey we are truly nearing the point of origin.

Living from the end

One of the great secrets is that we can wish for almost anything once we put our mind to it. Everything that exists today was once imagined. That is a fact. The house that you built was only once in your imagination.

But that imagination was so strong that the physical manifestation was just a matter of time. Let us explore what is working here behind the scenes. The first act comes from a thought. Thoughts are energy patterns but it will start to move when you add your imaginative powers behind it. You make a conscious choice to initiate a thought in your mind. That thought could be to write a book, for instance. Nice thought but so what? The next comes from our endowment of imagination, which is not available in animals. The imagination once awakened will stir feelings. You begin to "feel" the contents of the book and even see the finished product in your mind's eye. These feelings activate the subconscious mind, which is linked to the universal subconscious mind. The subconscious is not personal as it does not know anything else. As long as it is activated it will move other energies. If left alone the subconscious is on auto pilot, so you can make suggestions to the subconscious mind, and tell it that you have unlimited capacity to be what you intend to be. Go to a quiet place and approach this inner component of your life and begin to feel the reality of a thought. Feelings are powerful energy movers. You then begin to act on those feelings and start compiling your scripts. You start with one section and as you finish it you feel good. This will generate another level of energy and motivates you on. When it is aligned to source energy manifestation will take place. Things appear to fall in place for the book project. You offer gratitude for the arrangements and this feeds the subconscious to supply more. To the uninitiated these may seem to be pure coincidences, but it is really manifestation of formless energy to form. These feelings must move from the foundation of love as GOD is love. When you feel good, you are feeling God. Our intentions have to be sincere and congruent to higher dimensions to manifest a reality of fulfilling a wish.

Daily affirmations

When we want to connect with the highest self, we need to feel good. Feeling GOoD is feeling GOD. When we feel good, we are in a zone of bliss. These can come from thoughts that trigger an emotional response and here I offer my view of what can be your daily affirmations. Please feel free to develop your own affirmations because it is your expression of who you think you are in relation to the universe.

Where do I come from and who am I?

I come from an invisible realm, an unseen formless place which is from the most high.

I come from nowhere, and will return to nowhere when this physical time is up.

I am connected to the divine creation that gave me life.

I am thus from divinity, and I am capable of evolving into a divine character that is in resemblance of my creator who made me.

I am that I am

How do you see yourself?

I am a spiritual being having a temporary human experience

I cannot take my possessions when I return to spirit, so therefore need to be a giver, and not a taker

I seek permission to be of greater service to others

I am love and I am also peace, and moreover I am music that needs to be heard

I am a soul train that needs to explore all stations of life

What is my purpose?

I am here to be an instrument of peace and do God's work on earth

I am His voice to others who are seeking the WAY

I lived my life in accordance to universal principles and aligned to His wisdom so I can be His example

I am a piece of divinity and to connect with all others from the same source of being, as one

When we take the time and effort to connect with others on a personal level, we show the human side of us in our relationships and also the "being" which is the true identity. As an observer we can realize that many events that come before us are the run of the mill, what Lao Tzu names as the 10,000 things. These events and activities consume much of our time if we allow them to. Some are necessary but many are just distractions and are based on others wanting attention for their own fulfillment of earthly wants. Majority of the drama that unfolds daily come from again a fear based paradigm that others want attention to feel secure and be in control of everything (which is a projection of what could go wrong), thus elevating one's own anxiety unnecessarily.

Affirmations are our thoughtful declaration of our purposeful intent to the universe and when we can do this daily we make a pact to be in alignment to the greater scheme of things and a divine plan. Do this each morning as your dharma. We offer a morning prayer each day for a new experience and a gratitude prayer in the evening for the day that was unique as it will never come again. Each day is precious because it is one of a kind.

Coming home is a metaphor that allows us to come back to the point where we all started from, the formless energy that created the universe, and begin to know it for the very first time. Within the creative force we can learn an important realization that we are God like (or God consciousness), however we impose self limitations at the subconscious level. We need to have the courage and the passion to live life full and amplify the soul music for the world to know. Now that we have made a U-turn back to source living, we are ready to move into the next station of renewal and truly bask in the fulfillment of life. Enjoy the next 4 stations yet to come. They are meant for us to turn up the speakers and start the musical beat of higher living. We owe it to ourselves to celebrate these later landmarks of our existence with song in our hearts and soulful reflections.

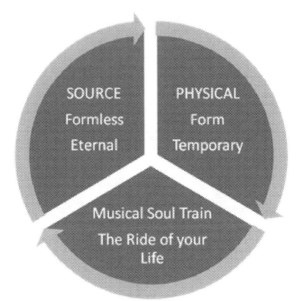

SOURCE
Formless
Eternal

PHYSICAL
Form
Temporary

Musical Soul Train
The Ride of your
Life

Station 9: Let the Music Play On

Quote:

Please do not die with the music still in you, for the world is waiting for your song to be sung

STATION NINE

Let the music Play on

Do not die with the music still in you. This profound sentence did strike my core. Yes indeed, why are we so afraid to let our music play, why are we so apprehensive to let the child in us surface. The world certainly needs more music and play time. Coming back to the domestication process, we have been led by well-meaning adults to behave more seriously and had forgotten to remember to have fun along the way. Let us start this reflection by looking at the 5 Regrets that give us a view of what we have let pass us by unknowingly and probably too busy to even consider or notice.

The 5 Regrets

To have the courage to live a true life, not what others expect of me.

Do what I am passionate about, and allow the flow, and believe that it will come together. Do it now, enjoy the moment as there is no better time. Be bold to pursue your passion. We often over-analyse the "what ifs" and creates too much internal dialog. Instead just be and allow things to unfold, as all happenings are an intricate arrangement. To do what makes me happier and not do just to please others. There are many demands on our precious time to fit another person's agenda and to suit others. We allow others to dictate how we spend our time. Be assertive but polite in refusing to give in. Allow others to also respect your time, as you respect others for what they want to spend time on. Never have a desire to control others. Release and allow others to be. Let go and let live.

I wish I did not work so hard.

Be aware that we need a balance, and not be blindsided by illusions. In the morning of life, this never entered our minds. Working hard was a statement of commitment and showing the boss we are an asset to the organization. I have no issues with hard work, but we need also to work smart. Very often we tend to "miss the children growing up years" and this can be a common trait. Burning the candle at both ends, and forgetting the important events is detrimental to your health and also your relationships. I know of one such person who placed his career above many other events, to a point when he retired, he made sure he made sandwiches for his son each morning to make up for lost time. Only difference is the son was already 22 years old and it was perhaps 10 years too late for the sandwiches to be made. Take time to enjoy, with right balance towards work and pleasure. Work needs to be joyful and not a burden. You can enjoy every moment by being totally present and not only be happy in the future. Happiness is the way, each and every day. View work as an expression of your love for your family.

I wish I had the courage to express my feelings more.

To say what I really feel and not say what I think others expect to hear and be honest to myself. Get to the point and avoid all the perceived drama. Tell others this is my opinion and they have the right to accept or reject it. In eastern cultures children are not encouraged to mix with adults and are probably asked to leave the room. Thus growing up we were perhaps less opinionated. Many times we fail to express our true feelings for fear of rejection or punishment. There should be a balance of courage and consideration. We are a product of our choices in life. Each choice comes with consequences, and be man enough to face the consequences that may come along.

I wish I had stayed in touch with my friends.

After leaving school how many of you keep in touch with classmates? If you have been in contact with them it is a good thing to do, then congratulations to you. If you have not, you are not alone in this predicament. Many times we move on and forget our true relationships until it is too late to make amends and have a failed EBA (emotional bank account). True friends are precious so make the most of it and remember those moments. Each encounter is to be viewed as a divine arrangement and this should be cherished. Be an active role partner in the building of relationships with another human being.

I wish I had been happier.

To see each day as a new beginning is a start in the right direction. Stop worrying about the "what ifs" and take whatever comes in your stride and do your best in each situation. Stop thinking ahead too much as tomorrow will unfold a new adventure and a great mystery and yesterday is history. Live more in the moment, the power of now, because this is the only time to appreciate and act upon. Happiness starts from the paradigm of what goes on around us. One secret is to adopt a state of constant gratitude and bliss.

Happiness comes from true health, meaning we are free from illnesses and able to have a full functioning physical body that has been endowed by God. The second part is being in harmony with everyone on the planet. Each one of us comes from the same source. Respect all of nature and all living creatures.

Having an abundant life, with all material blessings that are permitted to us should be cherished. Never waste God's gifts.

In addition, be in constant gratitude for daily happening, that are designed to show us a way and to teach us. How can we ever complain when we have already so much of material accumulation? We are hoarders. We own so many clothes that we only wear at most 20% of them. The rest are seldom touched, yet we still want to buy more. Bow down to receive and adopt a humble attitude. The more in life we succeed the more humble we should be. Take the lower seat and you receive great arrangements. Just like new tea that is to be tasted, you need to lower your cup so that the new tea (the wisdom and blessings) can be poured in. If you maintain being aloof, and your cup is above that of the kettle, you will never enjoy the tea. This is a simple explanation of the practice of humility. Humility is strength.

Accepting all of God's arrangements with gratitude and joy on a daily basis should be our mantra. Make a choice today to do things with fun and passion. Each day is a gift and we throw it away when we fail to make the most of it. Today's gift is tomorrow's history. ENJOY the PRESENT, it is God's gift.

Take a second look at the 5 regrets. Does anyone relate to some of them? The irony is that we are not even aware of them. Our busyness with the 10,000 things often gives us a false sense of accomplishment. How many are not their true self, but pretend to be someone else they are not. To the parents out there be careful when you want a son to be an engineer just like you, a successful engineer, or a daughter to be a medical doctor because you have been a successful practitioner yourself. I hear many a times, parents know best, and perhaps they do. All I am suggesting to you is to be mindful of this potential trend of thoughts. Your children may have come through you but they are not from you. They came from a greater source. They are unique beings and they deserve to let their music play to their own tune.

Enjoying the moments—let the music begin

I have come to the conclusion that there is always a reason to celebrate. Be it birthdays or anniversaries we need to find time to take hold of the moment to cherish and be merry. This is simply because "time waits for no man". If you missed your child's first steps you would have missed it forever. If you did not attend your son's or daughter's graduation, or celebrate your love one's 80th birthday, it is over. So have a desire to celebrate. It is so important to celebrate the moments. Many will brush it off and say it is not necessary, no need, it is always the same. As we get older no need to remind us of our age. Life itself is a celebration, so if we take a passive role, life will just be the same one day after the other. If this day would be your last, would you be sitting in front of the TV watching your regular soap opera, or would you be doing something else more purposeful. My advice is to take each moment to have fellowship and connections. It can just be a simple meal together but the importance comes from the thought and we tell that someone "you are special, and I celebrate this occasion with you". Those moments cannot be replaced, not in a million years. Moments are precisely what it is "moments". The joy of hosting a celebration for a loved one, just to see that "look" in their eyes for just a second is all worthwhile. The "D-day" of an event is the destination. The journey to that destination is what this is about. There is tremendous joy in the preparations, as it is love manifested by many who take part in the celebrations. Our family has its fair share to finding reasons to celebrate moments. Some memorable "moments" that we have had as a family includes:

My children's birth

My first born came in 1982, and there was an air of excitement. When my wife's water bag burst in the late evening we rushed to the maternity ward of the local hospital. As with all first born, "labor would be prolonged" and we were advised that I should go home and rest. They said, "it will be a long wait", so dutifully we listened after all who were we to question the so-called experts. When my son was born at 5am, I was fast asleep at home. Apparently they had rung the house but no one picked up the phone. Oh boy! So for the other two kids I made it an absolute point to witness both their entrances to the world. What a sight to behold. I am proud that I did not faint.

Our 25th wedding anniversary

Six months prior, I had made all the necessary arrangements for a surprise party to be held in my niece's condominium. Together with family and close friends, there were close to 50 invitees. My youngest son greeted us with champagne as we alighted from the lift to the pool area, and that was a moment to remember.

My son's graduation in Melbourne Australia

My eldest son graduated in 2002, and he was doing his finals in Melbourne, Australia. While on the phone he told us it was ok not to come as the travel cost would be pretty high, even if we did not fly 1st class. But this was not to be missed. He was the first one in the family to graduate and the entire clan went to Melbourne, all in 8 of us, including my sister, my niece and my sister-in-law. Money aside, it was a great 10 days of memories. To witness the graduation and by just being there, was worth it.

My 55th semi retirement birthday

This I must confess was my own personal surprise party for me from me, complete with live music and all, and of course starring yours truly and the musical soul train entourage complete with full range musical instruments, with a 5-piece band in attendance. The theme was "55-Oh", after the famed Hawaii Five-O series.

My sister's 70th birthday

You turn 70 only once, right? So off we went to an Italian restaurant, took over the entire 1st floor and surprised my dear sister. My sister is a retired teacher, Kirkby trained in the early 50s, and also an avid badminton player representing the country in the Uber Cup. It was nostalgic as we managed to get her badminton cronies, her school teachers and even tracked down her students. It was a great success with 100 guests in attendance. I even had a 3-piece band hired from Malacca all the way to the Italian restaurant. That is what makes the difference.

My brother in law's 80th birthday

You also turn 80 only once, and reaching 80 is an outright achievement. At 80 my brother in law looks 20 years younger than of his actual age, and all this is attributed to his love for sports especially swimming. We did a montage showing his youthful days and even his wife dedicated a song to him wearing a wig and all. Without a doubt the live band also performed, with modern and soulful music blaring on the airwaves. The nieces baked a beautiful cake shaped in the figure 80.

My alma mater Class of 72 40th Anniversary

Many left school and never met up. This event was held over 2 days of celebrations at a resort in Port Dickson. Some 25 classmates, many making the 10 hours flights from far away places showed up. We even had a football re-match and what a sight to see 50 plus white haired to balding homosapiens attempting to be sweet 17 all over again.

Our close friends' birthday celebrations

We had our fair share of hosting our friends' surprise birthday parties and the party planners (volunteers) swung into action right away. Some were smaller affairs but all were great surprises. You should marvel how they transformed a hall into a work of art. On all those occasions the music played on. These events allowed respective family members to pay tribute to the birthday boys and girls. What better way to celebrate and enjoy these good times when we can and not wait until we are dead stiff. No amount of crying does any good then. So never wait. Say what you have to say, create the moments to remember and you are a better person by doing it.

Chinese New Year and Christmases

For the last 20 years, we have held celebrations in our home, and mostly have been pot luck affairs. Great fellowship and good food and wine, what more can you ask for. We are truly blessed.

I wanted to share these stories with you to remind you that it is in our power to create situations, events, our power to do a deed, to serve others, because the joy seen in the face of loved ones and friends are a gem to watch. As you give joy, you attain a much bigger joy within you. The soul train lives on as we celebrate life itself. Cherished moments are indeed a gift from the high heavens.

As with everything else, all these celebrations are also temporary, but the moments that we take time to cherish is the key. This does not mean that we never do it because of its temporary nature. The very fact it is temporary, the more reason to do it more. In the ups and downs we encounter in life we must always find back our center, the middle path.

Even if we are in a festive mood for just an evening, it is worthwhile. Nothing lasts forever, be it joy or sadness, and these will become events that we have experienced, which mold us. What will be long lasting is finding the peace within yourself and the calmness that you can draw upon when the world throws its fair share of turbulence at you. You need to establish the "center" within you and you must work at it constantly to have it in place.

The next station allows us to explore this path and to find a place for contemplation and to meditate so we can emerge a renewed being each day. These sanctuaries are not of any religious intent but rather a universal principle of centeredness. It also reminds us that as spiritual beings in a human existence, we need to find that connection with the rest of humanity and to treat people based on the "whole person paradigm" of body, heart, mind and soul.

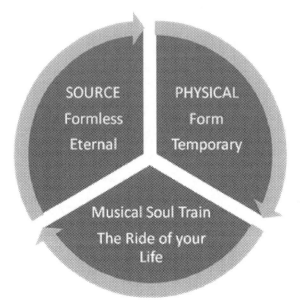

SOURCE
Formless
Eternal

PHYSICAL
Form
Temporary

Musical Soul Train
The Ride of your
Life

Station 10: Finding Your Sanctuary

Quote:

Every encounter with another person is a holy interaction, and we treat people as a whole person paradigm of body, heart, mind and soul

STATION TEN

Finding your Sanctuary

It is important to find a time and place for you to rejuvenate one self. The day to day events will consume you, draw your energy levels, and many of the 10,000 things that others wish to impose their will upon you increases your stress levels. You need to manage this effectively and find what works for you. There is no one answer. Some meditate while others do insightful reading of a book, some needing a quiet moment, and some go for long walks. Some sit quietly in isolation for specific time to just have time for themselves. Whatever is good for you, in that sacred place you take stock of how you are feeling, contemplate on what is your purpose, and be connected to Source energy. At these times, we need to also silence the mind to reflect and one of the suggested methodology is in the **Mind Platter** (details shown below), which allows what is termed as "connection time". The brain which is one of the most worked organs in our physique requires both up and down times in order to function and feel good.

Here I would like to tap on key learning concepts for self renewal from The 7 habits propagated by Dr Covey and the Mind Platter of Dr Siegel. Steven Covey gave the world two concepts for self rejuvenation which is, "Sharpening the Saw" and "Whole Person Paradigm" concepts. Let us now cover the 4 dimensions of life that needs equal attention.

The 4 dimensions see a human being as having 4 areas of life that need to be taken care of. You cannot short change any one aspect if you truly want a happy and meaningful life. The 4 dimensions cover the physical, mental, social/emotional and finally the spiritual aspects. Let us explore further each of the 4 dimensions.

Physical dimension—Body

This is the body (the outer portion) which has been given to us in its greatest perfection. To keep this work of art in the greatest of shape require us to exercise regularly and also have the right nutrition. The recommended exercise regime calls for aerobic which raises the heart levels and also for a minimum of 20 minutes for effect. For the older generation brisk walking 3 times a week is the minimum frequency required. There are many regimes to follow. Some go to the gym for a work out. Some have personal trainers. Others may take up a sport to their liking. When you are younger, possible sports are soccer, basketball, squash to name a few. In the twilight years many turn to lower aerobic exercises as the old bones and muscles are weak. Choosing one form and having the discipline is the critical factor. No investment no gain in the future. Food consumptions and adequate drinking water are also necessary. Nutritionist created the food pyramid, which are followed by many. This body given to us is a temple that needs to be looked after, and not to be abused.

Mental dimension—Mind

Our minds will stagnate if we stop exploring new challenges and engaging with others on meaningful dialog and also reading and meeting people to broaden your knowledge. Continuous study is an active activity as we are never too old to learn. The minute you stop learning is when you are six feet below. As long as the heart beats, we should be a magnet to learn new things. We have much to learn and just being aware where we are headed to on the final train ride back to origin, the source can be a totally new insight for many. The mental capacity to store and retrieve information is fascination in itself. Brain specialists have told us there are two main portions, with the PFC (pre frontal cortex), and the LIMBIC system.

The PFC is by comparison very limited to store past events. The PFC covers a small area on the frontal side and has small capacity in analysis and data retention. Because of its smaller make up, the data retrieval takes a longer time, and often we go blank. However the PFC is ever present in the moment, therefore we need to be fully conscious of where you are and what you are doing there. This is the CONSCIOUS part of our brain and we use it for the moment, the NOW moment. It allows us to make choices and then move forwards. For this reason, learning requires several repetitions before the data can be transported into the LIMBIC system. This is also our SUB-CONSCIOUS. All our past memories came from here. We must manage this and some areas are mentioned in Ho'oponopono teachings.

Social Emotional dimension—Heart

This is to connect with others at a level that provides us a connectivity link. We are social beings and we need social interactions to survive and thrive. We are not an island and we will perish if we are isolated for long periods. There is also the emotional bonding and building trust in your relationships. It is the key to maintain a positive EBA—"emotional bank account". Our spoken word and action, when done correctly and tastefully, making and keeping promises, will add positively to our EBA. This is because every promise kept increases your trust level with another person. On the contrary when we break promises, we withdraw from and lower the EBA. The EBA is like our money based accounts, the more you save, the more wealth you have, only difference in this case the wealth is in the trust bond you establish. Many fail to see this fundamental principle and often use people to achieve an end. This is a short lived and narrow view and does not go a long way. Touching hearts is the way to go.

Spiritual dimension—Soul

This is always the more sacred space and we belong to various denominations in religious beliefs. In addition it is also our alignment to universal principles like the Law of the Harvest and Law of Gravity. This dimension provides us with a means to connect to a higher power which is important in times of need. For many this becomes an anchor to weather the storms of life when you understand its connectivity to the source of all creation.

We are in an era of wisdom and many publications are already in mainstream media and there are many good wisdom books available today. This dimension covers the unseen but extremely influential in its applicability. Till today a fair bit of people are very skeptical as we were all born with the 5 senses that make our world real. Hence what we cannot see and touch is considered non existent here on planet earth. The truth needs to be discovered by each and every one of us. As with touching of hearts this deals in deeper realms which connects our spiritual relationships. Your faith and religious preferences need to be embraced to guide you along.

In the whole person paradigm model we have to see others with a view of body, heart, mind and soul. Our old views focus only on the body primarily, as we are hired for manual labor, and as time progressed, we tapped into the minds and asked for their opinion (which is also engaging the heart).

When we look after the 4 dimensions we become more balanced and live happier lives. In tandem we have the 4L's, that is to live, learn, love and leave a legacy. This provides a holistic approach to balance all the relevant aspect of your lives, and the bias is that you cannot neglect any one.

The MIND Platter

The MIND platter suggests that we have to make time for various mental activities that allows the mind to function at its optimum level. There are 7 blocks of time that make up a healthy mind. Again here the bias is that we pay attention to all 7 areas and not skip a few. See this as a buffet spread that we need to try out a bit at a time. All of us have only 24 hours at our disposal so we are on equal footing. However how we engage our brain (which is our main hardware) is crucial.

The platter covers the following:

- **Focus Time.** *When we closely focus on tasks in a goal-oriented way, taking on challenges that make deep connections in the brain.*
- **Play Time.** *When we allow ourselves to be spontaneous or creative, playfully enjoying novel experiences, which helps make new connections in the brain.*
- **Connecting Time.** *When we connect with other people, ideally in person, or take time to appreciate our connection to the natural world around us, richly activating the brain's relational circuitry.*
- **Physical Time.** *When we move our bodies, aerobically if medically possible, which strengthens the brain in many ways.*
- **Time In.** *When we quietly reflect internally, focusing on sensations, images, feelings and thoughts, helping to better integrate the brain.*
- **Down Time.** *When we are non-focused, without any specific goal, and let our mind wander or simply relax, which helps our brain recharge.*
- **Sleep Time.** *When we give the brain the rest it needs to consolidate learning and recover from the experiences of the day.*

The above concepts are just 2 examples of self energizers that are available to us and are sometimes not taken seriously until something breaks. These are similar to doing preventive maintenance for equipment to ensure higher uptime. When we tax ourselves obsessively chasing the worldly possessions, and forget that finding a sanctuary is equally important, we may end up to be too sick to enjoy the fruits of our labor. A sanctuary allows you to take a step back and clear your mind, body and soul (spirit) for a fresh start.

Some practitioners also do exercises on mindfulness by taking time off their hectic schedules to play it down, silence the mind and manage the stress. Depending on what you subscribe to, you can do a 30 second mindful exercise to a recommended 8 minute meditation. Others take time to do breathing exercise and even short spells of yoga. Some others like myself turn to music as an energizer. I play soft background instrumentals in the office and even at home when I read or do some writings. Many of these allow one to center back quickly and then move on. If not the daily grind will take its toll eventually with manifestation of diseases and symptoms such as high blood pressure.

For me, I also find an added sanctuary in my music studio that I go to almost every weekend. When I pick up an instrument and select a song to play I am connected to a different plane and I forget all the woes of daily living. In music you are immersed in a common language of love. You lose yourself in the primal rhythm that matches the beat of your heart and soul. Music does not rush you and you can dictate the tempo to your moods. You can choose from unplugged rhythms to jazz to ballads to new age. When you immerse yourself you feel the fluidity of the energy that pulsates into audible tones, which are again energy manifestations. You control what comes out from your imagination on what you need to portray in any given moment—soft ballads, upbeat pop tempo or jazz fusion. That is the wonder and flexibility of making music, and it reminds us of the tapestry of cultures and races that make up our planet's population, and how we can blend with another human being if we embrace this concept of connecting to their own music (their inner core). Music really cuts across boundaries and connects people. It is a cool experience. Life too should be a cool experience and it is in our power to make it so. Connect to the music in others. Encourage others to discover the song within them. Everyone has rhythm built in system. As long as your heart beats, you have rhythm and you got music.

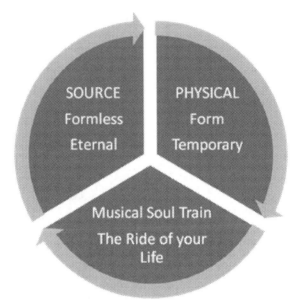

SOURCE
Formless
Eternal

PHYSICAL
Form
Temporary

Musical Soul Train
The Ride of your
Life

Station 11: Songs of the Soul

Quote:

Musical energy transcends all cultures and languages to touch the soul to show the way to the light and the truth

STATION ELEVEN

Songs of the Soul

The 11th station is somewhat a place of dedication to all those who have blessed us with the greatest of songs composed by great song writers of our times. I have selected several songs and lyrics, short verses, as a tribute to the song writers and artists who have graced this lifetime of ours. Listen carefully to the spirit in the words which are truly magical. Songwriters are truly gifted human beings as they put to paper words and musical notes that are their language of love and hope as spoken to the world on what can be a better place for everyone. Many write about their life experiences and most of them will connect ultimately to love and harmony and it is their personal quest for a better world.

These are my personal translations and interpretations of their messages from the mind of a self made musician, and I hope you can relate to them in your own lives and enjoy each reflection. I do encourage you to have your own connection to these pieces because no two minds are alike. We all have to find our own space, our own sanctuary and meaning of it all. Enjoy this musical trip down the strip with me. I find such magic in the lyrics that have been so carefully written and orchestrated.

Love Will Keep Us Alive

I was standing all alone against the world outside
You were searching for a place to hide

Lost and lonely, now you have given me the will to survive
When we are hungry love will keep us alive

Reflections: we can choose to be an individual person who believes that there is no need for others in this world. Everything you have achieved is based on your own intelligence, and efforts alone and you take great pride in your success. If you are in this state, consider that pride comes before a fall. The alternate view is that the minute we were born we were in the cradle of our parents arms. Even those who were abandoned, your foster parents gave you love and comfort. Yes, you seem to be standing alone, but there is a higher spirit that gave you life even before conception. This great love that came from source that created you in its magnificence in the 9 months of gestation in your mother's womb will not abandon you. The people who show up in our lives are not a coincidence. They were sent to love and comfort you. In turn we need to return the love, by loving ourselves so we are capable to give love, so we will never go hungry anymore emotionally and spiritually.

Daily affirmation: I am born out of love, from a place of great beginnings so I am love and capable to give love in abundance.

What a Wonderful World
I see trees of green . . . . red roses too
I see them bloom . . . . for me and for you
And I think to myself . . . . what a wonderful world.
The colors of a rainbow . . . . so pretty in the sky
Are also on the faces . . . . of people going by
I see friends shaking hands . . . . saying how do you do
They are really saying . . . . I love you.

Reflections: how can we say life is wonderful when there are so many people suffering in poverty and in a hunger situation, some on the verge of starvation. Surely we need to have some pity on them. Yes, for every act of suffering we also have many acts of kindness. You need to be the change that you want to see in the world as quoted by Mahatma Gandhi.

However you also cannot be in poverty yourself to help those in poverty. You cannot help a sick person by becoming sicker yourself. Rather than wallow in the pity realm of things, you should ride forward and be a beacon of hope for others. This means that you have to know what you are looking for. We all have a choice to make a difference, and the test is do we take that leap, or we stay in our comfort zones, because we are safe and contented. For every dark cloud, comes a rainbow. This gives us hope and faith in the greater scheme of things. We have to trust in the divine nature in all of us. When someone does an evil deed, it is not because he is evil, but he is moving away from source energy. Everything that comes from source is kind and loving and creates beauty. When we learn to love others, we make the world a better place. We see them as the creation of love and make attempt to connect and unite in love and harmony. When we come from this god conscious realm we will feel good, as we feel GOD.

Daily affirmation: Today I will learn something from nature, as one of my greatest teachers, to coexist in harmony with others.

Tears in Heaven
Would you know my name
If I saw you in heaven?
Would you feel the same
If I saw you in heaven?
I must be strong and carry on
Cause I know I don't belong here in heaven . . .

Reflections: when you lose a loved one, you hurt deep inside. These are the times you wished you had said what you wanted to say but never took the time to do it. We always say we have time later, but it never comes until it is really too late. So the lesson is "what are you waiting for?" Learn to appreciate those around especially loved ones. Tell them how you feel before it is too late. We rush through life in a dash and are always in 4th gear. We need to learn to slow down and really look around, and be present. Enjoy the time together and you need not shed tears in heaven, because you have lived a full life and together created heaven on earth. Be also the peace that you want to create. Do not look for peace but be the peace in you. When you truly subscribe to this and it becomes your flesh and blood, you will have made this planet a better place for others.

Daily affirmation: Starting today I will be like the sun that shines with warmth and love and never asks for a return of favor.

From a Distance
From a distance the world looks blue and green,
And the snow-capped mountains white.
From a distance, there is harmony,
And it echoes through the land.
It's the voice of hope, it's the voice of peace,
It's the voice of every man.

Reflections: our problems are problems because we label them as such. We argue over small things and make mountains out of molehills. This is coming from EGO consciousness, where we want to be right, win the argument and be first in everything. The world is a better place when we suspend the EGO which is edging god out, and away from what source energy is.

Today the world is not at peace. Pick up the morning paper and you see conflicts, wars and hatred between groups of people in many countries. Governments fight over an island. Neighbors do not talk to each other. Even family members do not even eat a meal together. Such has been society, with all being busy in their own little world. We can make the world a better place, and it starts with each one of us. There is hope for humanity, and it begins with love and sincerity. Ultimately peace is within us and we must share this peace with all who we meet and harmonize with nature.

Daily affirmation: There are no problems in the world. We label them carelessly and fail to see the opportunity hidden within.

Imagine

Imagine there's no heaven, it's easy if you try
No hell below us, above us only sky
Imagine all the people, living for today
Imagine there is no country, it isn't hard to do
Nothing to kill or die for, and no religion to
Imagine all the people, living life in peace
You may say I am a dreamer, and I'm not the only one
I hope someday you will join us, and the world will be as one

Reflections: some of us today live very blessed lives, while for some, it is a constant struggle, if you are in a country with conflicts and civil unrests and each day is lived one day at a time. With such comparisons can we ever have a heaven on earth? The reality is that both heaven and hell is right here. We need not see it as a place to go when we die. We are taught from the time we could walk that we need to fend for ourselves, and charity begins at home. We go to school and study hard and to graduate with a degree so we can secure a good paying job. We see the world as a competitive environment, and we need to fight for each piece of pie since there is only so much to go around. This is where those who live with a scarcity mindset will have a (give me) attitude. When competition and conflict become a common behavior, we have manifested a hell-like living, and there is no trust. As a contrast an abundant mindset will also allow others to have their share and will never fight for more. Ever been to a buffet meal and observe how some react. They will take piles of food on their plate because they have already paid for it, not thinking that waste is also a sin. Many will have this attitude and we need not join the masses. If we are of the thinking, what can I possibly do, as a lone person, it does become a high order to influence change. The spirit of doing the right thing does not need the masses to change in a relatively short time. If we can be an example to just one more person, we have done our fair share. As the song goes, we can always dream of a better world and having one more person to support the cause is all we can do, one at a time. We need to re-connect with each other so as to be united to secure our future existence.

Daily affirmation: Do not ask for peace but be the peace that you want the world to be.

The Prayer

I pray you'll be our eyes, and watch us where we go
And help us to be wise, in times when we don't know
Let this be our prayer, when we lose our way
Lead us to a place, guide us with your grace
To a place where we will be safe
I pray we will find your light, and hold it in our hearts
When stars go out each night remind us where you are
Let this be our prayer, when shadows fill our day

Reflections: I have eyes but cannot see, I have ears but cannot hear, I have a mouth but cannot speak. When we were younger we relied on our parents and well meaning adults to lead the way, to protect and show us the path of life. We grew up in a safe environment and while we did not know the world, our loved ones protected us from what they would have perceived as negative influences.

As we matured we became more independent and started the search for a guiding light to find out who we really are. As we walk the pathway of wisdom, we attempt to see beyond the obvious, to feel beyond the physical and be touched by a divine energy that serves as our guiding light as long as we open our hearts to it. This path we seek will elude us if stay on an EGO conscious level because we attach successes solely to our personal efforts. When we let go and allow GOD into our lives, we will feel the light and love. We can climb mountains literally when we combine our efforts with GOD's power.

Life as we know it has its waves and nodes. When we are in alignment to source we will be guided to a safe place, in the sanctuary of love and harmony. Even in what we perceive as our darkest hours there is always a guiding light to find our place of peace and live in God's grace. When we surrender to the divine intervention, we will ride the waves with gratitude and survive the nodes with high resolve to serve humanity and God's children. When we have the faith, we will always be in his grace.

Daily affirmation: In my darkest hour I may be lost, but my internal light shines forth to reveal a hope for another beginning.

Amazing Grace

Amazing grace! How sweet the sound
That saved a wretch like me!
I once was lost, but now am found;
Was blind, but now I see.
Twas grace that taught my heart to fear,
And grace my fears relieved;
How precious did that grace appeared,
The hour I first believed.

Reflections: this classic piece has graced many places of worship, homes and concert halls with its sweet and soulful rendition by the greatest of artists. Here we give thanks to the blessings we receive more than we care to acknowledge. Our human failing is taking everything for granted and we have a mindset that the world owes us, not knowing the world was here first and we are actually only the visitors. We all came from an all encompassing source of infinite wisdom and upon conception we did nothing in our mother's womb and yet everything was done for us. Everything that we needed for life, from the eye brow to our heart beat was all ready in that microscopic dot, where a thousand could have appeared on a pin head. Yet all that wisdom manifested and ultimately multiplying into our 60 trillion cells is truly awe inspiring. So when you feel lost and alone, tap into this divine energy that is within you and be saved. Believe and you will connect to the source of all creation. If every cell knows its calling and fulfils it, we too have the same capacity to reach higher limits. When we make efforts, divine presence will do its part. The grace will come forth the hour we start believing.

Daily affirmation: With the grace of God in my every step, I will not fear to start a new beginning.

Smile

Smile, though your heart is aching.
Smile, even though it's breaking. When there are clouds in the sky, you
*   get by if you smile.*
Light up your face with gladness.
Hide every trace of sadness, although a tear may be ever so near.
That's the time you must keep trying.
Smile, what's the use of crying
You'll find that life is still worthwhile, If you just smile.

Reflections: in life we experience joy and sometimes sadness. The state of joy and happiness is much easier to handle, but when we are challenged with negative emotions such as fear, sadness and disappointments, we find it hard to swallow. When we are faced with life's roller coaster ride we have two choices, we either wallow in the negative energies and sink even deeper or we rise up to the occasion and tell ourselves we will hold our head up high and start anew. As the song lyrics suggests the sun will come shining through. The sun is always there, but sometimes just hiding behind the dark clouds. As one door closes, another one opens up. We have to be courageous to move forward and not dwell in the past. You can never change the past and thinking of what could have been is not helping anyone especially your own self. You have only the present moment to make a choice and move on to the next action. With all of life's turbulence we will still see life as still worthwhile and invest in the future.

Daily affirmation: We are sunlight children of the world. So smile courageously.

The World as I See It

The world as I see it, is a remarkable place
A beautiful house in a forest, of stars in outer space

From a bird's eye view, I can see it has a well rounded personality
From a bird's eye view, I can see we are family
It's not hard for me to love you, hard for me to love you
No, it's not a difficult thing

Reflections: we live on planet earth and this is our only home and the only one that can support life. No other planet has been able to support the human existence. This must have been designed for a purpose. From a distance I can see it as perfect, no wars, no crime, no conflicts. If we can be more tolerant of each other this world can be a wonderful place. However, EGO drives us against each other. We fight over territorial rights for a small island, we quarrel over small issues, we have to be right all the time. Learn to be detached from the world of 10,000 things, which are trivial and often unimportant. Learn to see each other as our own family, because in essence we are from the same source of creation. Because this world is our sole platform for sustaining life, we must protect it from extinction and promote environmental awareness. This movement should never be politically motivated but from one concerned earth citizen to the next. When we live in harmony the world indeed becomes a beautiful place. Learn to love each other, learn to love nature and learn to love our only planet for human survival, for us and the future generations to come.

Daily affirmation: Each morning as I watch the sun glow from a distance to light up my world I remind myself that this view has to be preserved for all of eternity.

Well there you have it. These are the several works of amazing song writers and how they have shared with us their inner thoughts as they see the events of this world. I hope you manage to connect to some of my personal favorite musical selections. The words reflected are truly inspiring and magical and it allows you to peek inside their deep thoughts of what is to be a better world for you and for me. It is often difficult to put these thoughts and concepts across in a normal conversation, but when you do it this way embedded in a musical medium it reaches people far and wide and it seems so natural to play it. And because it is recorded the messages are molded for eternity. That is the power of song writing and singing these songs in your heart will make each day a new beginning and the joy of being alive. Not only merely alive but to live in "XO" (extraordinary) land, which is an extraordinary existence which is your birth right to own.

I would like to complete this section with a simple song that everyone knows but bears a clear message that we are responsible for our own life and destiny and it is up to us to make this path we choose to be on purpose. All of you know it and it goes like this:

- *Row, row, row*—this tells us that we need to take action. As we conceive thoughts, we must put them into steps that we commit to take and move steadily forward. Do not let the memories of the past hold you back, as from this moment on the future is in front and we can only go forward. Results will stem from actions, as the great Einstein once said, nothing ever changes until something moves.

- *Your boat*—YOU have to be the one to change things around you. This is your life (your boat). Do not row somebody else's boat or the boats that others wish you to row. Row your own boat. This is your life. Take charge and take responsibility. For things to CHANGE it begins with you. Do not wait for others to take the step, as you can never control them. You can only control your own decisions.

- *Gently*—be kind to yourself, as you will falter along the way but do not despair for all good things are always at the end of the tunnel. Look for that light, which is in you waiting to spark. In everything that you attempt, just put your best foot forward. That is all you can do, to be true to yourselves that you have given the best you can.

- *Down the stream*—go with the flow of things, do not move up the stream against the current. Be like the nature of water, that it is gentle and obedient and yet powerful. Our ego gets the better of us and we want to win every battle. Some days we may lose the battle, but not the war. This says we need to attain higher awareness and wisdom to navigate the waves and nodes of life. All obstacles are designed to test us, just like the rocks and rapids, the whitewater, before we can reach a serene section of the stream. Behind every challenge lies an answer.

- *Merrily, merrily, merrily, merrily*—enjoy life's journey each moment. Each day is brand new and perhaps an opportunity will present itself to you and unless you recognize it, it will pass you by. Life is temporary yet it is on purpose and we have a mission to fulfill so be joyful and in gratitude for the blessings we receive to allow us to function each day. As you endeavor each day whether in your work or at home, do it with joy or not at all.
- *Life is but a dream*—YOU make it as you see it. Develop your own end in mind vision of how you have lived your life and the legacy you choose to build. Do not stop dreaming as dreams are meant to fulfill your dharma. You are destined for greatness in your own unique way and do not let anyone tell you otherwise. Do your best this very moment this day, as today becomes tomorrow's history and it is already a dream of days gone by.

We have travelled far and contemplated many new insights for us to consider and as we approach the final station, we have earned a well deserved stop at the peak to soak in the heavenly wisdom, as you now have realized the vast potential that is available to us all to be or not to be, that is the question. As we journey on we may feel that we have been here before (to the point of origin where we actually started) and begin to know the place for the very first time, as we see it with renewed eyes and a shift in perception. A new reality awaits us and it is up to us to embrace it.

SOURCE
Formless
Eternal

PHYSICAL
Form
Temporary

Musical Soul Train
The Ride of your
Life

Station 12: Extra Ordinary Living

Quote:

We may not be able to do many great things in this lifetime, but we can do small things with great love

STATION TWELVE

Extraordinary living

Thank you for following my journey this far and using the music of the soul to guide us.

To give a perspective of the great musicians of the world and how they touch our lives, let us explore a little further. It is not only a matter of being technically competent to train on their musical ability but to have a sense of moral responsibility of giving oneself to humanity. When we reach satori (the awareness in closing the gap between us mortal souls and the realm of God's will) it is to realize that we owe a debt to the world, as we have disturbed the harmonious rhythm of the world with conflicts, pollution and environmental exploits. We need to offer sincere apologies and make efforts to stop the further deterioration of planet earth. Each person has a role to play, even a small part is helpful and like an orchestra, we will be able to immerse ourselves into the music (our dharma or our calling) we play and to combine body, mind and spirit in oneness which is pure to the heart. The highest level of satori is to merge and be what the divine presence is and that simply means to be what God is. When we can be at this level we are truly oneness, and no more a duality. The 7 faces of God as depicted and taught to us is the essence of creativity, beauty, love, kindness, expansiveness, abundance and receptivity to all of creation. If you ever wondered what a God-like virtue would be, these 7 faces give us a clue to the secret domain of the highest creation.

To live responsibly is to be accountable for our words, actions and thoughts which are lacking in the world today. Many are doing incorrectly and chasing wealth in a robotic fashion and have little comfort of true accomplishment at the end. They may gain fame and fortune but not the spirit of an extra-ordinary life. We should be a role model to ourselves, our children and society. Our number one job is to change ourselves so that we are better than who we were before, and leave this place in a better condition then when we first stepped foot on. The Japanese word for human is *ningen*, where nin = person and gen = space. We are here not for our own purpose but in relation to those around us, the space that we are connected to. A true human is to live in harmony with your "space", which is everything that you are in connection with, your world and all others in it including the plants, trees and animals right down to ants and micro organisms. When you reach this point of awareness you are only then truly worthy of been a human being. The "being" which is the true self becomes the guiding light where the human, the physical aspect will eventually follow in actions. The purity of "being" is likened to the top of a waterfall which has to be pure so that water downstream is also pure. When the upstream water is polluted the downstream is muddy. When our being connects back to source spirit which is divine in nature and of pure intentions we live in accordance to the principles that encompass creation, love, beauty, kindness, expansion, abundance and openess to other beings with whom we share this space called earth.

When we harmonize with the rhythm of the universe it is like singing a duet from our hearts. Sharing a song need not be in front of crowds but can be done even in solitude, in the forest, by the sea as long as the spirit is right, and it comes from deep within us in giving our best without expectations of reward or getting something back. This is truly giving of ourselves and is the greatest virtue to adopt as part of life itself. We come with nothing and will return to nothing, so it is meant to be giving. This is the WAY, the eternal greatness of the TAO that will guide us each day if we allow it to.

As the train begins to pull in to this last station of this human adventure, let us remind ourselves that we owe it to ourselves to be living an extraordinary life. It is merely a thought away. Master your thoughts and you will change your life. Thoughts are powerful vibrational energy. Thoughts start on how we view things. Thoughts are high level energy patterns, much faster than light and sound.

As you think so shall you be.

Start today to migrate from ordinary levels of human awareness to a higher level of awareness. Ordinary levels of awareness stems from domestication of having a good education, a good paying job, settling down with a family and enjoy the years before your return to source. There is nothing wrong with this, but you will not want to settle for less when there is potential to be on a higher plane, where you find true purpose and meaning and answers the question of "who am I, where did I come from and where will I be going".

This means the way we see, our paradigm makes up our world, our reality. We base our perspective on the form and boundaries established by man and Lao Tzu refers to this as the 10,000 things. For the most part, rules and boundaries are man-made and this is an illusion in many cases. You can witness this in the various cultures of the world, where in one is possible and in another prohibited. We also often label problems as what is perceived in our heads. I remember a phrase that said "a problem is a problem if you call it a problem, but the problem is not the problem itself, rather the way you react to it becomes the real problem". We tend to label events as good and bad, when in reality it is neither. We just choose to label an event based on our thinking and followed by our reaction after the thought.

How do you see your life each and every day. The great Einstein once said that you can see the world and each day as nothing special and there are no miracles or you can choose to see that everything around you is a miracle. It is a perspective that you choose to have and both are equally true as long as you frame it as such. For example you can see the world as everything is not enough to go around (a scarcity mindset), or there is plenty to go around (an abundance mindset). Do we see people as generally good, or all are crooks. Challenge your thinking, be mindful of the power of your thoughts, beware of the domestication that leads us to label actions that come from past fear based events.

You are responsible for the way you think. That is the fundamental responsibility you have to realize. Each moment we think negatively we will have internal parasites growing and it robs us of our peace and happiness.

Learn to be in the moment, the NOW, that is the only time you have influence over, not tomorrow and not yesterday. It is at this moment what you are thinking and feeling that is important.

Every action comes from a thought. Each thought comes from inner understanding of the matter or perception, real or otherwise. It stems from a belief system engrained when we were taught as a young child, and these emotions are all stored in our subconscious mind. Many past actions are replayed automatically from this level and we relived those moments again and again. Someone who you do not like, triggers an automatic emotion in you whenever that name is mentioned, even if that was 10 years ago. We simply cannot let go. But we must if we want to be happy!

Secondly, have a personal mission in life and live out your passion What am I here for, who am I? Am I spirit, or this is all there is based on just my 5 senses. What is my purpose of this existence and where do I go after I die. It may be difficult at first but once you step aside from the daily 10,000 things and spent quiet time and contemplation, it will dawn on you. Have I fulfilled my dharma, my purpose for which I was brought forth to do here. Surely I can partake in God's work and this will be my greatest gift and my commitment to be his voice, hands and legs to manifest a heavenly civilization. How do I know what my mission is? Just start from the roles you hold. If you are a son, be the best son that could ever be. If you are a mother, be the best mother you could ever be. If you are a manager, be the best you can be. Ponder and research yourself what it means to be the best because nothing is more meaningful until you achieve an insight on your own and not what others tell you. You have to reach deep in your thoughts and meditation for the answers.

Determine how you liked to be remembered, what is your legacy. This vision does not mean any arrogance on our part but as a way of thinking from the end to fulfill our purpose. It starts with the role you play with various people you associate with as being a father, brother, son or mother, sister or daughter. Work at each role, and be mindful and vigilant how you are progressing in each of the relationships.

Also work on what brings joy to you, and what are your natural talents you can use to express your inner being. Once you are able to realize and capture this, what we call your element, start to live it through with passion, for what is more rewarding than doing something that you absolutely love. And getting paid for it is a bonus. Bring out that passion, live your dreams, and not what others want you to do. Perhaps you always wanted to be a painter, or write a book or be a dancer. Follow that dream. It is never too late. I waited over 50 years to write a book and I am doing it today. I am living that dream.

We are all a victim of domestication and we are told early in life to study hard and get a good paying job, not what you like to do. Being a drummer or a professional dancer does not put food on the table we are told, in a no nonsense manner, so we do not find our true calling, our true passion or element. Look around you, how many parents send their kids to do arts and music as compared to those that levitate towards the sciences, medicine and business areas on accounting and economics. Simply because they have greater means of higher earning power. We are often driven by the money equation. I am not saying those are necessarily wrong but are these vocations their true calling. A further reading by Dr Ken Robinson's book entitled **The Element** is a good pick to understand this subject a little more.

Build a relationship that lasts.

Everything we do involving others is always an interaction, and what better way than to see each encounter as a holy divine arrangement. It is not a question of whether we like a person or not, as some will not be as kind or as accepting, but they are our greatest teachers because they push our internal buttons, sometimes to the limit. It is not about them but how we choose to react wisely is the key. When someone cuts into your driving lane, you cannot control their actions, but your own reaction to that situation. If you get angry and say foul words, we are misaligned to the vortex of light and truth. Getting angry does not affect that driver one bit, but your anger builds up toxins in you which are potent enough to kill an elephant. So watch your emotions and feelings the next time you are tested. We have to see the divinity in all of God's children. Mother Teresa has taught us to see the disguise of Jesus (divinity) in every human even in the depths of poverty in the streets of Calcutta in India. Of course we are not Mother Teresa, but we can do our small part in not judging others and avoid foul languages being spoken.

Once this radical view can be accepted we will have a new paradigm with all of humanity as how God sees us all as his children. You then would have become a trusted individual whom others feel connected and can rely on your word, because it is who you are, someone trustworthy and is capable and competent in your chosen field of specialization. Your trustworthiness is a combination of your competency (specific skills) and character. All these qualities take time and effort to master and mindful nurturing to build up our EBA, the emotional bank account, one person at a time. Every interaction we have with another person is an opportunity to develop a lasting bond, and see this as a holy encounter with another being of the highest creation out of the divine source. When we can reach this level of insight we are on song and in alignment with the harmony of the universe.

You begin to see that there is bliss when there is synergy in motion where people collaborate as a well knitted team, complimenting each other, celebrating their differences to which the power of the team will surface. Be a solution provider and a team player. We see this reflected in team sports everywhere. The individual blends in with others to become complete, wholeness and oneness. There is no separation. There is only one. The spirit of the team is one. The self is subordinated and the team takes center stage. After all who are we but as part of the divine equation leading to pure love and harmony to be offered among all men.

Be a giver to life and life will turn out to be better for you. As we came from no where to now here and finally return to no where, we will never take one particle of our possessions with us when we die, so stop all accumulations in an obsessive manner.

Be of great service to humanity. Be like the great source which you came from to be a giver and be in a state of abundance. Once you can do this it will bring so much joy, not only for others, but for you as well. This joy raises your serotonin levels in your body, and you feel good. Also others who witness the act of giving will feel good too. Be like nature, who always gives and asks nothing in return, be like the sun that shines with warmth and love each day. A love like this will light up the whole sky. Be like the plants that are designed to release oxygen and absorb carbon dioxide from the air through the photosynthetic function of its leaves. Do you know that an average human adult requires 53 liters of oxygen per hour at rest, and we need 400 small plants (with approximately 30 leaves each) to generate that amount of oxygen that we need. By default we are always takers and nature is a giver. We were designed to be one with nature and thus we can learn so much from it. Sadly man is today destroying nature for material gains, and this is contrary to God's laws.

The mentality of an abundant person will start the flow moving and you can then be a wellness recipient of the universe's love. The natural laws will respond in the same vibrations as you give to it and you will be a vessel to receive such blessings. Learn to be generous.

The degree of generosity, progresses from a lower level of thinking that "**I have to give**" to "**I need to give**" and at the higher level of awareness, "**I want to give**". Ultimately, "**I get to give**", the highest level of realization as this comes from the abundance mindset and state of gratitude feeling that we have more than enough and we can share. When we can give more it means we are in that position to do so and instead of having a EGO trip, we should be thankful that we are allowed to be a giver. We can always give $50 to a more needy person, or a smile to a stranger. It need not always be a gift of money and materials but a gesture of kindness goes a long way.

Each day ask of yourself, "How can I be of service?" As a leader in your organization, explore the concept of a servant leader, and ask of yourself what can you do to help your people do their jobs better. Do not micro manage them and get in their way. If you do they will always wait on you for instructions and they will never grow. As all great leaders do, create a vision and establish some clear boundaries and then get out of the way. Your people know more in their own field of work and you need to encourage them by creating the space and unleashing their talents, which are their songs waiting to be sung. As a parent, ask yourself if you are allowing your children to be who they are, and not what you want them to be. This poses a big challenge to many parents who by their own upbringing never saw this new way of thinking. After all they followed what their own parents wanted, so why should it change? By all means be there to guide them when they are young but as you teach them the values, you have to trust and little by little release them to the world. After all you will not be here forever, so you need to let go.

Animals do that to their young, and almost directly after birth, young off-springs start their worldly journey quite independently on their own. Only humans cling on and we become too possessive with the excuse that our children need us to be there to guide them. This is all made up in your own mind. The more you control the greater they wish to be free. The more you dictate the more it will fall on deaf ears. The more you judge the further apart you drive them away. Parents need to learn to balance their roles as parents and be just a friend at times. I have seen 20 year old adults who are still being referred to as "my baby" because parents cannot let go of that image, that although your child was once a baby, that physical body of the baby is no longer around as he has transformed into a young adult. Our physical body has changed in form and structure. This physical attachment has to be managed in your mind. It is time to let go.

Each day you can also make a practice to give something away, be it a kind word, a small gift, a smile, an appreciation for job well done, a patient ear, a non judging remark, a few dollars to the needy or even buying a stranger a cup of coffee. There are many ways to be a giver. Try this for a week, then a month and then for 365 days and watch your own emotions as you do it and observe the miracles that will unfold before you. Challenge yourself to do this. It can be life changing because we are by domestication always a taker, what is it for me and charity begins at home principle. Learn from nature which is always giving and supporting each other. When the tree withers it returns to the soil as fertilizer for other plants. Plants give out oxygen to support life, and we human needs lots of good air as basic need to survive. Livestock are slaughtered as food meat for consumption by humans. Fruit trees bear abundant variety for our consumption. Man has always been a taker and it is about time we start doing the reverse. We accumulate possessions to a point that it becomes obsessive. When you understand that less is more you have truly understood the temporary nature of all things we attract ourselves to and which we take absolutely nothing with us when we return to source.

Leading wisely

When you are in position of power, it is very easy to let your EGO dominated-self get the better of you. In the industrial age thinking the boss is seen as superior to all and he gives the orders. Only he is able to think and others do exactly what they are told, basically follow instructions. To be a true leader you need to live virtuously and that is to display the following qualities of great leadership. Here again the great Lao Tzu guides us with his wisdom and for all those in power especially in large organizations and in government these qualities serve as a reminder for us to govern well. The term "leader" role is also referenced towards parents, teachers and educators of our younger generation who will one day be in the position to lead others. There are four qualities of leadership suggested here.

The first is to be like a valley under heaven.
A valley is normally fertile land with streams and is able to nurture growth. Nurturing is what farmers do in tending to their crops and they get down on their knees to scoop up soil to plant seeds. Farmers fully appreciate the Law of the Harvest, that the crop is only as good as the

seed you plant and the love and care you offer during the growth period. If you neglect this you will not have a bountiful harvest. You can never rush the seed to germinate and it takes its natural time cycle to sprout. There are no shortcuts. Planting is also an act of humility when you go down on your knees to the eye level of the soil. Although you possess a given title you need to have this heart of humbleness in the manner you lead others. After all you are all the same from the act of creation, which is our Source. You are just playing a given role.

The second is to be the pattern for the world.

Great leaders do many things starting from their visioning and aligning of resources to achieving their goals. The lasting virtue of a great leader is to be a pattern which means you need to model your virtuous behavior in front of your people. This comes from building your character base which is the foundation of your being. It is like the strong roots of a large tree that bears fruits and holds big branches. This strength comes from the unseen, that which is below the ground level, but where the potential energy flows from. Only when you become the pattern for the world will you be able to truly lead from the front. Your modelling comes from the natural and sincere inner you and you dismiss any ego patterns. Character ethics include integrity, honesty and the will to succeed. Respect is given to those who display the competence (skills of their profession) and the character ethics (behavior) in their daily actions. When you flow from your authentic self it lights you up as an example for those you lead.

The third says to act in accordance to eternal power.

You need to have the vision to move your people forward but at the same time undertsand when is the right time to step back. While a general can give orders, he is wise enough to know that the man on the field, his trusted lieutenant knows the terrain better than him, so he lets go. It is an act of release rather than one of control. When you understand this concept you bring out the best in others because you demonstrate that you believe in the higher potential in those that you lead. At the same time you never abandon them as you take accountability for their actions. You are like a fountain that pours life continuously into a pond that allows the fishes to be what they are meant to be. A great leader surrounds himself with people who are smarter than him in their realm of expertise, and this builds up a powerful team. Same with a parent, you nurture a child in their formative years but know when to step back and allow the potential of your child to be what he is best at doing and not to impose your will as you may think you know best, but is never true. Leading is a role that you play for the moment it is needed. It is never a right to possess. Mindful leadership knows when to play a lead role and when to step back. As one of the great CEO's of the modern era, Jack Welch, once said, "my job is to create a vision and then get out of the way".

The fourth says to preserve your original qualities

What were those qualities before you even took shape in the physical space. This draws us back to the time of creation and the formless energy that is eternal. In the power of intention we speak of the 7 faces of God. If we were to think as the highest source what would that be. That is what we need to return to and this will include creativity, love, kindness and beauty to name a few, that defines your essence. This view gives a leader the perspective that while we are all connected, we need to respect the varied qualities in those we lead. We are not isolated and we come from the same beginning and eventually return to the oneness of the universe. So lead with that inner reflection that we are one and each member on your team deserves the love and respect from you.

Irrespectively whether you are on your own or you take on a role as a leader of men, living virtuously is an essence of the true being, encompassing a heart of humility, being a God-centered role model, building the character ethics and having the child-like qualities to live spontaneously, being in the moment and enjoy your vocation. Life is meant to be lived at such an extraordinary level, and everyone has a right to claim it.

Live each day to the fullest

I used to take each day for granted and there was always another time and day to do things. While I do not profess to have mastered this fully, I make it a point to remember it as often as I can that each day is special because once passed it will never be repeated. What you do in this present moment is gone forever the next instant. As I gathered material for this book, new thoughts were quickly captured on paper as those thoughts may not come again. It is like opportunity knocks once and then it is gone. When I placed pen on paper I captured the moment of thinking and for that I am very grateful for such insights that come at the right moment. It is a magical experience. Some days you can stare and nothing comes to mind that is worth capturing in words. In the writing of this book I find so much joy to record new insights which flows to me, often in the early quiet moments in the mornings. As it comes it reinforces my own learning experiences and realization that the wisdom is always there for us to tap in to, and for this I am eternally grateful.

I recollected a reading from Steve Jobs, in a three-part speech that he gave to graduating students and the last part was about death. Steve was diagnosed with cancer and he was staring death in the face. Sometimes some event like this suddenly makes you see the world in a totally different perspective. Below is an extract of that speech he made:

When I was 17, I read a quote that went something like: "If you live each day as if it was your last, someday you'll most certainly be right." It made an impression on me, and since then, for the past 33 years, I have looked in the mirror every morning and asked myself: "If today were the last day of my life, would I want to do what I am about to do today?" And whenever the answer has been "No" for too many days in a row, I know I need to change something. Remembering that I'll be dead soon is the most important tool I've ever encountered to help me make the big choices in life. Because almost everything—all external expectations, all pride, all fear of embarrassment or failure—these things just fall away in the face of death, leaving only what is truly important. Remembering that you are going to die is the best way

I know to avoid the trap of thinking you have something to lose. You are already naked. There is no reason not to follow your heart.

It is very easy on a daily basis to get caught up with the nitty gritty small things, and we get upset when the train comes late, or the traffic crawls at 5 km per hour all the way home, or the dinner cooked for you is not good enough (too salty), and a host of other things. This calls for us to take stock of how we view everyday living. In a book entitled, **Tuesdays with Morrie**, which is about a dying professor who spends his last days with a former student and how each area of life is viewed as he relates them. He talks about all the events we take so much for granted from daily living, family, love, marriage, money, our fear of getting old, about forgiving others, living a perfect day and of saying goodbye. There is much wisdom to be learnt from this and to practise them while we are able to.

When we face death, all EGO denominated fears as the above article says, falls onto the wayside. What we had seen as a potential threat to our position or even a perceived embarrasment by not accomplishing a task is suddenly very insignificant in the larger scope of life. Only when we learn how to "die", can we truly learn how to "live". This is a fascinating concept.

The "dying" part is of the EGO, the big self centered view of who I am based on my possessions, position in the company, big titles, corner office and the company expense accounts and cars, not forgettng the jet setting on first class or God forbid, business class travel. EGO says we are our own person and everything we have accomplished is due to our own efforts and with no help from others. Is this really true? When we kill off the EGO we begin to see that we are all part of a bigger picture, that we come from the same source of creation and we will go back to where we came from. We will take with us absolutely NOTHING—no money, no property, no titles and no accomplishments. That is the reality and the sooner we accept this new view we start living life anew with humility, gratitude and awe inspired reflection of the great arrangements we encounter along the way.

What we may have accomplished is not within the human comprehension. We may work all our lives and still be having little money. Does that equate to success or otherwise. Carrying on with the speech Steve talked about the aspect of facing death in the face, as per extract below:

No one wants to die. Even people who want to go to heaven don't want to die to get there. And yet death is the destination we all share. No one has ever escaped it. And that is as it should be, because Death is very likely the single best invention of Life. It is Life's change agent. It clears out the old to make way for the new. Right now the new is you, but someday not too long from now, you will gradually become the old and be cleared away. Sorry to be so dramatic, but it is quite true.

Your time is limited, so don't waste it living someone else's life. Don't be trapped by dogma—which is living with the results of other people's thinking. Don't let the noise of others' opinions drown out your own inner voice. And most importantly, have the courage to follow your heart and intuition. They somehow already know what you truly want to become. Everything else is secondary.

Indeed your time is limited. Therefore on a daily basis, give thanks upon waking each day, and ask that you may be able to serve today to the best of your ability. Just do the best you can and move on. Live your dream and not the dream of others of what they think is best for you. Who really knows what is best for you? Do not be taken in by opinions of others. They may mean well, but they are seeing the world from their eyes, what I call their domestication paradigm. You have also been a victim of this process and that is why you need to break free and never take any views of others personally. Even when they praise you do not take it personally. Do not misunderstand this point. Not taking it personally does not mean we ignore the person and be sarcastic or be arrogant. We can be gracious and respect their views but your own center has to be established through a greater and stronger inner core. By all means acknowledge the compliments but do not get swell headed as if you are the higher superior person. We are not better than anyone else. We can only be better than what we were yesterday. When we are emotionally affected by other's opinions whether good or otherwise we are dependant on an external factor to feed our emotions, which is always temporary. One day your boss praises you and you feel elated, and another day he may ignore you and you feel neglected. Observe how our emotions play on us. Fascinating but so true in many cases. So do not take anything personally. Stay principally centered.

Putting this into practice means you do good deeds even when no one is looking or even know. Do it because it is the right thing to do, and not because you want to show others you are capable or seen to be taking action each moment. Pick up that piece of paper on the floor. Be a person who is one of high character and competence. Be one that people who may want to follow. Do it and feel good. Be an example by your deeds and actions. No need for high publicity and fanfare. Just be and be silent. That is the way of the TAO.

Finally, no matter how much you earn, spend less.

An extraordinary life requires us to be financially disciplined. Treat all materials preciously as these are given by the creator, therefore commit to stop waste and buying excessive stuff.

If you look around we are a wasteful society. We buy way too many things, we have clothes that fill three cabinets, have three cars each, and the list goes on.

Mastering money, and not let money rule you.

Understand that it is not what you earn but what can be saved. There is a simple difference between a rich and a poor man. A rich man saves and spends what is left and a poor man spends and saves what is left. Just a little twist in their approach and it makes a whole lot of difference.

Money is a form of energy that we use to secure what we need for a comfortable life. What is then a comfortable life? A roof over our heads and having three basic meals a day is a blessing. All others are luxuries. We get an education and is able to earn a living. We need not chase for more things than what we really need.

Do we really need so much? Even when we have a lot of money, does it allow us the right to spend it recklessly? Apparently there is a law in Europe that you can be fined for wasting food. I read an article that a person ordered so much food that half of it was left untouched. The restaurant owner called the authorities and the person was given a fine and a warning. The reason given was that, although money is yours, but the resources of the land belong to society. So wasting food is wasting resources that are meant for us all. We all have a responsibility to conserve scarce resources. What an insight!

Being healthy and in harmony with others and with nature is already a path towards true happiness. Prosperity is a measure of what we have based on our means to earn and is to be treasured. Be in constant gratitude for what we have. Money is only good when you do good with money, meaning it should be used for the betterment of others, not only for your own benefit. Money comes from the creator and we are permitted to earn it, so it does not belong to us. We are only a temporary custodian, and this life is also a temporary one.

Because life is temporary, do not take yourself too seriously. Please do your best but at the same time, be kind to yourself, and acknowledge the divinity that is a big part of you. You are the conductor of your orchestra and the world is your stage. Use it and fill your world with music from the soul. Keep safe and keep well. May the soul train within you continue its journey. We are honored that you have stayed with us till the end. God bless all those who have hopped on this ride with us.

Approaching the end of the journey

To add a touch of divine insight as an appropriate closure to this gracious journey called life, allow me to share with you the 25th verse from the Tao Te Ching, written by Lao Tzu, the great sage from ancient China, some 2,500 years ago which embodies what we all have in us which is the potential to be at our highest self, and may you seize the day to be the one that is *"Living from Greatness"*.

The 25ᵗʰ Verse

There was something formless and perfect
Before the universe was born
It is serene. Empty.
Solitary, Unchanging.
Infinite, Eternally present.
It is the mother of the universe
I call it the Tao

I call it Great
Great is boundless
Boundless is eternally flowing
Ever flowing, it is constantly returning

Therefore the WAY is great
Heaven is great
Earth is great
People are great

Thus, to know humanity
Understand earth
To know earth
Understand heaven
To know heaven
Understand the WAY
To know the WAY
Understand the great within yourself

The above 25ᵗʰ verse has been acknowledged as one of the greatest reflections ever conceived in Lao Tzu's writings from the Tao Te Ching.

It has a clear message that we are beyond average and beyond ordinary. This is not said in arrogance and with an EGO driven mindset. We are not this body that we occupy, which is temporary but deep within lies an eternal force that was never really born and thus will not die. It was there before we were conceived, and was formless, yet present and vibrating. As the final paragraph tells us, if we tap into this greatness, we will see the greatness manifest in ways beyond your ordinary comprehension. People will show up that are important for you, arrangements will be made for you, opportunities will surface unexpectedly, money will be made possible for your projects, which is what the law of attraction is when in motion. Trust in your own greatness, and also see the greatness in others. Be silent and tap into this reservoir that is in all of us, contemplate the voice that resides in the rhythm of the soul. Practise silence daily in your own sanctuary and observe the renewed energy and clarity of mind and be able to navigate the 10,000 things more effectively that may otherwise consume us if we let our guard down.

Allow me to again stress the point of trusting the unseen and the all powerful source of being, as we have all grown up fully educated and domesticated all this time to use our 5 senses of sight, hearing, touch, smell and taste to perceive our reality. I too have had my struggles to go beyond this thinking because of my own domestication and I do not profess to have mastered it but I am more keenly aware when my trust level goes down because the universe gives me signs when I do that. The messages will come in the quiet contemplation upon deep reflection and not in the rush of things. In the beginning it all seemed hocus pocus and I admit it takes time, exploration and even prayer to acknowledge this other side of greatness, the invisible realm of energy source. I am learning more each day myself when I am open to more experiences with gratitude in my heart. We often overuse our minds and think too much not knowing we only see a fraction (less than 2%) of what is really going on around us that affects our lives. Be mindful that your body functions each second without you ever thinking about it, the 60 trillion cell mates work on auto pilot to provide a full functioning human body. You do absolutely nothing in your mind and yet everything is done for you. Think about it, it is truly fascinating. So think less and allow. Stop controlling and release. Let go and let GOD in. I myself have experienced seeing new opportunities that arise when I close one door and another door opens. This is the trust that we need to cultivate and leave no doubt and as my great teacher once said, you have to have a knowing.

As I have progressed on the last 15 years in this soulful journey I am now able to appreciate more the law of attraction and how it really works. There is such a fine line between what we want and what we do not want and how we feel it when communicating these desires as we launch them in our thoughts to the universe. It is like having to control how smoke travels and what winds will blow to influence the smoke. That fluidity is so immense that the slightest iota of energy mismatch that takes place the whole momentum of intent shifts accordingly. That is the power of fully trusting and knowing, with absolutely no doubt whatsoever when you make a thought and take an action. The 25th verse calls this Greatness as boundless and ever flowing and is constantly returning, like a swirling mixture of intention and manifestation in an evolving cycle.

As the writings also suggest, there is a trinity between heaven, earth and people (humans), and each has its own greatness that will manifest to be in unison to establish a heavenly civilization. Between heaven and earth, God choose man to be His partner to do His will on earth what He could not do in the physical form, and that is to create a heavenly place for all of His children to live in harmony and prosper for eternity. In the study of the age of civilizations, we have seen the progress through each of the ages and we have come very far to have what we have today. Because of the material abundance and vast progress of science, industry and technology, we can enjoy the modern comforts today and we may have overlooked or perhaps taken for granted God's gift to humanity, and thinking that what we have achieved so far is due to purely human effort alone. Throughout history we have seen many sages (divine souls in human form) being sent down to guide us humans but we continue to go astray, which is contrary to God's law. When we understand the mission of humankind in the divine plan we will be able to match His will by creating a society that will have purity of heart and a loving inner nature for all things, so that all wars and conflicts will be eventually eradicated. Until we close this gap between the EGO conscious driven actions of society where the rat race thrives on for self benefit and material gains, we will not be blessed with the arrangements to flow with the WAY, the truth. Mankind needs to make a drastic U-turn of his materialistic and self centered pursuits and the disharmony between fellow humans and with nature, and to return to be God conscious in our daily thoughts and actions. We are running out of time as the clock for repentance (convulsions seen in unprecedented natural disasters around the world) has started already some 50 years ago and we are reaching the peak of baptism. How do we reconcile the fact that in some countries people are starving while other countries are burning wheat just to preserve the price level of this precious commodity. Same goes of the culling of young chicks because there is an over-supply of chickens and will affect the protected price level. This is wasteful in God's eyes and we call this progress. This has to change and we need to be the light and peace that we all want in this world. It begins with one person to change our attitudes and then to help another see the truth and do the same. We all have a mission to save ourselves from extinction and to preserve and sustain this beautiful place we call home. This planet is all we have. There is no second alternative. Unless we stop wasting resources, stop polluting the environment and learning to love and forgive another human being we will meet our faith and we shall all perish. Knowing this we must do our part to make the difference because we can only start with us, no one else. Do it now. We are on the path of extinction.

We have been on a long ride and have stopped and experienced each station of life and now reached the 12th station of the mountain. I thank you for taking this train ride with me so that I could tell my personal story and share the wisdom the great teachers have taught me. I am humbled by the wonderful experiences that cross my path and continue to learn each day. This is not the end of the journey because there is no end. There will always be the next 12 stations of life, and when our heart tells us, we get on board to continue the journey. This is a metaphor that there are many more wonders that will unfold before us, and as long as we are open to each day with gratitude in our hearts and an adventure in our souls, we will encounter many more stations. We need to constantly reach a higher level of awareness so that we are able to discover the true path and be that trusted confidant that the higher laws have endowed upon us because we are connected to the source of all creation and are capable to manifest actions for a better world.

As you close this book my sincere wish is that each one of you will discover your own soul train and play that music that is ever waiting to surface and be connected once more to the original qualities that was there even before you were born. For those who are already singing their unique song to the world, please continue on that path and I owe you my gratitude for being my soul mate and to have made this journey together and to have made this world a better place when we eventually leave it to future generations. You owe it to yourself and those dear to you to reach the peak of fulfillment and true happiness because this is your birthright. The 1st station is waiting for you. It is always there, and you just have to want to go there and get started. Enjoy the experience and see you at the top of the mountain. Bon Voyage.

The Final Connection

With all the 12 stations behind us after a long haul we end up staring in awe at the twilight sky as darkness falls over us at the 12th station and we ask if the journey has indeed ended. Well in a way the physical journey has been well explored and often we have also had references to the other side of the unseen realm, the mirror of our reflections along the path. While we are still alive in this body we seldom think about the "other" side as this is deemed taboo, because no one likes to talk about death when we have so much living left to do. In many cases, death is seen as an end to life, and even though it is a certainty, we forced ourselves to ignore it for as long as we can. In reality we need not fear death as we only return home to the maker, which is our eternal being that was never born and thus could never die. Those that pass on in their sleep or even with a heart attack are blessed to have not suffered for prolong periods before the final train ride is over here on earth.

In the final connection is it necessary to embrace the trinity of the spirit, the mind and body that makes us wholesome and we seldom realize these connections and take for granted that these matters will take care of itself somehow on a purely physical level. Little do we realize that the unseen realm has great influence and this concept entails an upstream and downstream connection in everything that we do and is around us. Everything that flows downstream (its final manifestation) comes from a higher source. This source is the upstream. Everything comes from the source and this is transformed to all physical manifestations we see around us today.

The wooden chair that you are sitting on came from a tree that came from a small seed a long time ago. Imagine walking into a furniture store to buy a chair and you are given a seed. Imagine the seed is that source, and over time it has transformed itself where we needed wood cutters and skilled craftsman to harvest the tree and make that chair. The spirit of that chair was already in the seed and the mind and body came after it. If it was a bad seed there would not have been any chair made. Everything starts with a spirit pattern that is already there before transformation takes place. So the concept of spirit first which is the formless prevails long before we have a physical representation.

Similarly in the family circle the upstream source are the parents and downstream are the children. The values held by parents and demonstrated in daily actions and words are captured by the children who observe each moment. There is no better teacher than by one's example. If the source was contaminated by disharmony between husband and wife, what would the natural consequence be for the children. It would be a home without love and respect, and they will pick up these negative habits as though it is a natural consequence of being a parent one day. They see and learn, wrongly or otherwise.

In an organization the upstream is represented by the virtues and conduct of management and the CEO. Many organizations embody a code of ethics in their company policies. A piece of paper will not mean anything if the actions of the top people are in violation to the code. If some bypass checks and balances just because they say so, it will lead to further consequences. Many fraud cases have been revealed because the same people who instituted the controls and were entrusted to protect its well being had violated them. The downstream effect is felt and there is no more pride in the people if they cannot even trust those who lead them, and some may have lost a means to earn a decent living altogether.

In government, the top leaders need to work for the well being and quality of life of its citizens and not take advantage of one's position for self gain as you are entrusted to serve those who have elected you to office. Only when we have conscious leaders who lead from the heart and not only from the head, who uphold the highest values and execute them firmly, will the positive effects be felt by the people for the good they do. Everything starts from a righteous spirit to serve and then you have policies and procedures that are in place to bring about a just and prosperous society and eradication of poverty. The people and country, which represents the downstream, become more prosperous from the great efforts of a clean and pure leadership, which is the upstream.

In dealing with nature, the upstream comes from the protection and conservation of the environment. When money and greed step in, we violate the laws and do massive deforestation and hunting animals to extinction. All these action disturb the natural balance of the planet which had been designed to ensure perpetuation and continuation. These acts will cause natural disasters to take place as nature attempts to undo the wrong and we as humans get the brunt of it. When upstream is contaminated by our actions we see the downstream effects.

Therefore our thoughts need to be pure as these translate to feelings and then actions. Pure innermost thoughts as upstream are important to be withheld constantly. When we perform deeds for others, if the intent is for self gain, although the action take place but the overall effect is detrimental in the final analysis. This is simply because when the expectations are not met the action will stop. However when we do a deed because we want to, and there are no preconceived expectations, that deed will last because it feels good. The act of giving is one that allows us to be on purpose, as we have said throughout the entire book, we came from no-where with no-thing and we will return likely with no-thing as well. The transition point on this earth is only temporary so all things physical like money, property and titles are never permanent.

In conclusion placing spirit first tells us to set the "unseen" pattern before anything else. The purity of this pattern will flow to the mind, our thinking and feelings in our body and then the actions. Pure patterns yield pure actions. Impure patterns have the reverse effect. When you harbor a pattern of revenge or hatred, your mind and body generates toxins and if you manifest that thought into harming someone or breaking something, you will answer for it eventually. When your source comes from love, all actions will flow with eternal goodness and acts of kindness will follow.

I would suggest that we begin each day with a prayer. It is an upstream action thought and sets a pattern that the prayer is a petition to the divine source of all things. How you set that pattern is also important. Gratitude and apology should precede any prayer for self purpose only. Prayers should be followed by actions that ride on the will of the prayer. These are examples of setting the spirit pattern, and the mind follows and the body belongs to. This trinity of spirit-mind-body is sacred and is a 3-dimensional cross like many others that exist in dimensional harmony. We have the sun-moon-earth connections in a 3-dimensional cross, and others such as father-mother-child, organization-leadership-people, and health-harmony-prosperity as some examples of the trinity of the cross.

The Mirror Effect

Mirror-mirror on the wall—to begin to appreciate and to validate the spiritual and physical realm as a back to back mirror of each other is fundamental and there are many situations that show us this mirroring effect, and below are a few examples to illustrate the point:

How you look at other people is a reflection of yourself—if you can see the good in others, it is in you too, and if you find fault in others, they are your faults as well. After all to be able to recognize something you too have had it in you at some point of time. If someone is rude to you, it shows that you too have that trait and that like attracts like. It is a message to change over a new leaf as an awareness of the need to do it. Therefore every person who is placed there to push your button is designed to teach you. It is sad that many fail to capture the essence of the training, and instead make judgments.

If you see possibilities in others and their potential to be more than what they are today, then you too have this potential, because you operate from a realm of abundance thinking and treat others accordingly. When you can see beauty in everything, there is also beauty in you. The world around you is a reflection, which is a mirror that shows you as the person you are.

Never blame or complain as it only makes matters worse. What is happening is a mirror that you need to reflect upon, because for things to change you have to change first. You need to take responsibility for whatever is happening in you to attract such events that caused you to complain in the first place.

Be a giver and in turn you give yourself a gift of realization that you were blessed in the first place to be able to give. Give unto man as you shall also receive as St Francis's prayer embodied this verse. See the creative wonder in nature and others, and you too will have the creative power within you to do a unique deed. This goes against the grain of conventional thinking where it is a survival of the fittest and you have to fight for what is yours.

Death is also a mirror of life. When we "die" we are born in the astral world and our ancestors will rejoice, while on this physical side loved ones will be saddened with the departure of the body. This is no more than a transition and death/birth happening simultaneously and when we have an astral death, a baby is born into this world. That is the cycle of life.

In the final analysis love others and be loved, seek to understand so as to be understood and listen with your heart and your voice will be heard. Teach others with passion and you will learn, and trust in the Lord, and your faith will grow. Take every event, people you meet, adventures that you encounter and even the heartaches, as a true learning platform as all things that happen are never a coincidence. It is wonderfully arranged and we either learn from it or we miss the golden chance for reflective guidance. God uses these people to send us a message.

To conclude on the final connection, we have to acknowledge the presence of divinity that gave existence to everything we have on the planet and have the gratitude in our hearts that we are very blessed and we have been provided for in abundance. This becomes the foundation of true prosperity when we are eternally grateful for everything and anything that comes our way. Keep this acknowledgement in your heart as you make your own personal journey on the musical soul train of your life. Be at peace always.

The trinity of spirit-mind-body and heaven-earth-humans is the universal alignment of upstream and downstream connections

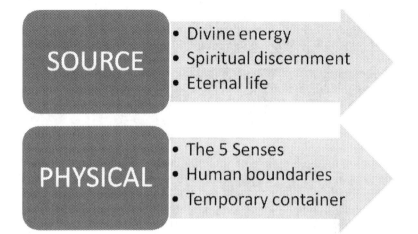

SOURCE
- Divine energy
- Spiritual discernment
- Eternal life

PHYSICAL
- The 5 Senses
- Human boundaries
- Temporary container

The Spiritual and Physical domain is a mirror of each other and the manifestation of events on earth has been energized earlier in the world of spirit

Source, Spirit, Main Soul - God's realm of infinite wisdom and truth

Mind, Mental, Choices that are generated from inspired thoughts

Physical, Body, Actions, Tasks that manifest are aligned to source spirit

When the upstream (soul spirit) is clean then the downstream (mind and body) is also clean. Our thoughts that come from inspiration transforms to impeccable words and actions that manifest physically.

Acknowledgments/ References

To Dr. Wayne Dyer in his teachings from all the books that I have read and the numerous PBS specials he has delivered in published videos.

To the great authors of books who have shared their insights and wisdom, including The Power of Now, The Divine Matrix, The 4 Agreements, Zero Limits and Teachings of Ho-oponpono, The Work, The Teachings of Abraham (Esther and Jerry Hicks), the 7 Habits and Zen Guitar.

To the great song writers of our times and whose music have filled my heart and the messages that you have given to the world to make it a better place for humanity.

To my close friends and colleagues who shared my soulful journey and given me the strength to believe in this path and the quest to explore even more with them.

To my family who have given me the opportunity to be who I am, as a husband, father, brother and an uncle, as the roles that I have taken on as a human being in my relationship with them in this physical journey, and believing in me as I have believed in them to be better persons than we were before.

To the readers and soul mates out there who share the same energy field and have inspired me to inscribe these personal reflections of life and the wisdom that have taught me to be who I am today.

About the Author

Born in 1955 in Malaysia, 2 years before the country's independence and studied in Pasar Road Primary School and La Salle PJ secondary school till the age of 17. Studied accountancy after leaving high school and worked in private sector for 40 years working with several multinational companies specializing in Financial and Cost Management, Business Strategic solutions and Process Management and spent the last 15 years researching and developing study material on human philosophies and spiritualism to answer the elusive question of "What is my purpose" and "Who am I". He has been truly blessed to find so many wisdom teachers as soon as he opened his mind to this quest and was a ready student to the teachings. He had developed a passion for music at a young age playing the violin formally and then as a self-taught musician on the guitar, keyboard, drums and conga till this present day. He visits his studio regularly and finds bliss in this sanctuary each weekend. Married blissfully to Regina with their three children, Terence, Tracy and Tony and now living in Subang Jaya, Selangor, Malaysia, some 25 km from central Kuala Lumpur. Philip found his passion for teaching in the mid-term of life, primarily in corporate leadership, financial management and later in executive coaching assignments. With new insights that helped bring more meaning to his training techniques he has used various universal principles to drive home core messages and is always ready to share the musical soul train journey with anyone who is open to explore a more happy and joyful life. He continues to explore new horizons in daily prayer and keen contemplation to carry on this amazing continual journey of life with the grace of God.